THE
FOUR
SEASONS

Tyndale House Publishers, Inc.　|　Carol Stream, Illinois

OF

MARRIAGE

GARY D. CHAPMAN, Ph.D.

Visit Tyndale's exciting Web site at www.tyndale.com

TYNDALE and Tyndale's quill logo are registered trademarks of Tyndale House Publishers, Inc.

The Four Seasons of Marriage

Cover design by Rule29.

Author photo copyright © by Boyce Shore & Associates. All rights reserved.

Designed by Ron Kaufmann

Edited by Dave Lindstedt

Library of Congress Cataloging-in-Publication Data

Chapman, Gary D., date.
  The four seasons of marriage / Gary D. Chapman.
    p. cm.
  ISBN-10: 1-4143-0020-4 (hc)
  ISBN-13: 978-1-4143-0020-7 (hc)
  ISBN-10: 1-4143-0023-9-(sc)
  ISBN-13: 978-1-4143-0023-8 (sc)
  1. Marriage—Religious aspects—Christianity.   I. Title.
BV835.C4575 2005
248.8′44—dc22   2005009145

Printed in the United States of America

13   12   11   10
7   6   5

To my wife,

Karolyn,

with whom I have shared

the four seasons of marriage

for more than

four decades.

CONTENTS

❦

PART I

The Four Seasons of Marriage

❦

PART II

Seven Strategies to Enhance the Seasons of Your Marriage

PART III

Putting Your Plan into Practice

PART IV

The Four Seasons of Marriage Study Guide

Notes

ACKNOWLEDGMENTS

I am deeply indebted to the hundreds of couples who participated in the research that preceded the writing of this book. These couples not only took time to complete the research questions, but were also willing to be honest about the quality of their own marital relationships. I have changed names and places to protect their privacy, but I could not have written the book without their help.

The basic concept of the four seasons came from my longtime friend Jim Bell. Thanks, Jim, for what has turned out to be a great idea. Ken Petersen and the professional team at Tyndale House have been extremely supportive and helpful throughout the process of research and writing. I especially want to thank Dave Lindstedt, who served as the editor for the project. His suggestions greatly enhanced the manuscript.

I am grateful to Tricia Kube, who computerized the manuscript; Shannon Warden, who collected and analyzed the research information that came to us via our Web site; Kay Tatum, whose technical expertise made it possible to meet publication deadlines; and Karolyn Chapman, who read the manuscript with the eye of an English teacher. Without their help, I'd still be scribbling on the rough draft.

I also want to express my gratitude to the many couples I have counseled over the past thirty years. With their permission, some of their stories appear on these pages. My life has been enriched by everyone with whom I have walked through the seasons of marriage.

INTRODUCTION

The tall and stately elm outside my window is covered with snow today. It's late January and winter has arrived in North Carolina. Schools are closed, as are most businesses, and the streets and lawns are swathed in a beautiful blanket of white. In the cozy comfort of my study, I sit by the fireplace and reflect.

I remember the summer we first moved to this place. Across the yard, the elm tree was engaged in a life-and-death struggle with a kudzu vine. The broad-leaved kudzu was winning, choking the life out of the hapless tree. Looking down the creek, I saw other trees that had already succumbed. Their dead limbs had fallen and their trunks, still pointing to the sky, were covered with snaking vines. They were simply waiting for the next strong wind to topple them.

Although I had arrived too late to save those other trees, I was determined to rescue the elm. With my sharpened, steel vine cutters in hand, I attacked the kudzu with a vengeance, circling the tree and severing every vine in sight. The larger ones were two inches in diameter, and the smallest was half an inch. Finally, I retreated from the battle and waited for nature to run its course. Within a week, the kudzu leaves had shriveled, and I imagined that the elm tree was breathing easier.

Summer soon faded into fall and fall into winter. When spring came, the elm tree put out its slender leaves in happy defiance of the gray tendrils still hanging limply over its branches. By the time sum-

mer rolled around again, the dead kudzu vines had fallen and the elm tree had a new lease on life.

Since then, I've watched the seasons come and go. I've seen the elm drink up the spring rains, soak in the summer rays of the sun, relinquish its leaves to the winds of fall, and cloak itself with white beauty in winter.

Today, as I sit here by the fire, gazing at the winter portrait outside my window, I'm also reflecting on the seasons of my life and my career as a marriage counselor. I'm thinking of the forty-two years that Karolyn and I have lived together as husband and wife, and I'm reminded that we, too, have passed through many winters, springs, summers, and falls.

I once heard a speaker say that there are four seasons to marriages. As he explained it, we begin as young couples in the springtime of life, excited about the future. Then comes summer, in which we become involved in vocations and perhaps child rearing. After summer comes fall, when the children leave and we are alone again. Then, in our latter years of life, we experience winter. Although there is some truth in this analogy, it seems to me a much too simplistic description of marriage.

My experience, both in my own marriage and in counseling couples for more than thirty years, suggests that marriages are perpetually in a state of transition, continually moving from one season to another—perhaps not annually, as in nature, but just as certainly and consistently. Sometimes we find ourselves in winter—discouraged, detached, and dissatisfied; other times we experience springtime, with its openness, hope, and anticipation. On still other occasions we bask in the warmth of summer—comfortable, relaxed, enjoying life. And then comes fall with its uncertainty, negligence, and apprehension. The cycle repeats itself many times throughout the life of a marriage, just as the seasons repeat themselves in nature.

The purpose of this book is to describe these recurring seasons of marriage, to help you and your spouse identify which season your marriage is in, and to show you how to move away from the unsettledness of fall or the alienation and coldness of winter toward the hopefulness of spring or the warmth and closeness of summer. The seven strategies laid out in the second part of the book will not keep your marriage from experiencing fall and winter; but they will give you positive steps you can take to make the most of each season, prepare for the next, and advance your marriage into spring and summer.

The seasons of marriage come and go. Each one holds the potential for emotional health and happiness, and each one has its challenges. The key is to develop the necessary skills to enhance your marriage in all four seasons.

Unlike trees, which are at the mercy of the weather and other factors, as humans we have the capacity to make decisions. We can choose attitudes and actions that will improve and strengthen our marriages. We can plant seeds of love and hope in the springtime that will produce fruit during the summer. And we can harvest a storehouse of good feelings and open communication that will prepare us to weather the changes of fall and the icy cold of winter.

If you have picked up this book in the dead of winter in your marriage, take courage. There's hope. I have watched hundreds of couples apply these strategies and experience the "blooming of the crocuses" in their relationships. I believe that these practical steps will work for you as well. Even if you're reading this book alone and your mate is not willing to participate, I will show you how to start on your own to win back your spouse's heart and move your marriage toward a warmer season.

If your marriage is currently in spring or summer, it's important not to let the kudzu vines gain a foothold in your relationship. I will show you how to cut the tendrils of negative attitudes and actions and free your marriage to be all that God designed it to be.

If you find the book helpful, I hope you will share it with your married friends, who are also experiencing the four seasons of marriage.

PART I

The Four Seasons of Marriage

THE NATURE OF
MARRIAGE

In the early days of my career, I was an avid student of anthropology. During my undergraduate and graduate studies in that discipline, I explored ethnographies compiled through the years by various anthropologists. One conclusive finding of these studies was that marriage between a man and a woman is the central, social building block in every human society, without exception. It is also true that monogamous, lifelong marriage is the universal cultural norm.

Of course, some people will deviate from this practice, as in polygamy (which is still found in a few nonliterate cultures) and serial monogamy (which has become common practice in some Western cultures), but these exceptions do not erase the cultural norm of lifetime monogamy from the human psyche. In fact, in spite of the widespread acceptance of divorce in the United States over the past forty years, a recent poll of never-married singles ages twenty to thirty indicates that eighty-seven percent planned to marry only once.[1] Many of these people have seen their parents divorce and that is not what they want for themselves.

The social institution of marriage is first and foremost a *cove-*

nant relationship in which a man and a woman pledge themselves to each other for a lifetime partnership. In the biblical account of creation, God's expressed desire is that the two "will become one flesh."[2] At the heart of marriage, therefore, is the idea of *unity*. It is the opposite of *aloneness*. Again from the creation account in Genesis, it is abundantly clear that God did not intend for men and women to live alone.[3] Something deep within a man cries out for companionship with a woman, and the woman has a similar desire for intimacy with a man. Marriage is designed to satisfy this deep search for intimacy. Thus, marriage is not simply a relationship; it is an *intimate* relationship that encompasses all aspects of life: intellectual, emotional, social, spiritual, and physical. In a marriage relationship, a husband and wife share life with each other in the deepest possible way. They view themselves as a unified team, not as two individuals who happen to be living in close proximity. Because the desire and drive for intimacy are at the very heart of marriage, the individuals involved become troubled about their relationship when such intimacy is not attained.

Marriage is also a *purposeful* relationship. All research indicates that an intimate marriage provides the safest and most productive climate for raising children, for example. But procreation is not the only purpose of marriage. Each person is also endowed by God with certain latent possibilities. The partnership of marriage is an ideal environment for nurturing and developing these gifts and abilities. As the writer of the ancient book of Ecclesiastes observes, "Two are better than one . . . If one falls down, his friend can help him up. But pity the man who falls and has no one to help him up!"[4] Every married couple has experienced the reality of this principle. Two are better than one.

Husbands and wives are designed to complement each other.

When the man is weak, his wife is strong; when she stumbles, he is there to pick her up. Life is easier when two hearts and minds are committed to working together to face the challenges of the day.

THE ESSENTIAL NATURE OF MARRIAGE
Committed
United
Intimate
Purposeful
Complementary

After forty-plus years of marriage, I look back and realize that many of the things I have accomplished would never have come to fruition were it not for the encouragement and help of my wife. I'd also like to think that she has accomplished more with her life because of my support. This brings me a great deal of satisfaction. Together we have committed ourselves to seek and follow God's plan for our lives. We help each other discover our unique giftedness and encourage each other to use these abilities to serve God and to promote good in the world. As we do this, our lives point others to God and we accomplish our highest end. Our marriage relationship enhances the effectiveness with which we serve God.

King David captured the vision for us in Psalm 34:3: "Glorify the Lord with me; let us exalt his name together." From a biblical perspective, the purpose of life is not to accomplish our own objectives. The purpose of life is to know God and to bring glory and honor to his name. For most people, marriage enhances the possibility of achieving this objective.

ADAPTING TO THE CHANGING SEASONS

Marriage relationships are constantly changing. Attitudes shift, emotions fluctuate, and the way spouses treat each other ebbs and flows between loving and not so loving.

Sometimes, change is beyond our control. For example, when Ben's wife, Nancy, was told she had cancer, the diagnosis changed the fabric of their lives and their relationship. They could adapt to the situation, but they couldn't control it. The same was true of Tricia and her husband, Rob, a member of the National Guard. When his unit was activated, he was sent into a war zone half a world away. Rob and Tricia could adapt, but the circumstances were beyond their control. When it became clear to Jon and Carol that her mother could no longer live alone, they had to respond to a change that they couldn't control. Life is full of unanticipated changes. Our only choice as couples is in how we will respond.

Other changes we create for ourselves, but sometimes with unexpected consequences. When Ken and Melinda moved to Kansas City after living near her family in Chicago for ten years, it created numerous changes that they now had to face together. The decisions we make regarding vocation, child rearing, education, civic and church involvement, and other areas of life create changes that affect our marriage relationships. The manner in which couples process these changes will determine the quality of their marriages.

In the natural world, the four seasons are created by certain inevitable changes that occur as the earth turns on its axis and revolves around the sun. Likewise, the changes we face in life (and the way we process and respond to them) create the seasons of marriage. The birth of a baby, the death of a loved one, illness, in-laws, getting a job, losing a job, the demands of a job, travel, vacations, weight gain, weight loss, financial ups and downs, moving, staying, depression, disagreements, moods, teenagers, aging bodies, aging parents, hobbies, habits, sex, impotence, infidelity—all these are examples of situations and circumstances that put pressure on a marriage and demand a response. If we respond well, in harmony with our spouse, we can keep our marriage in spring or summer. If we don't respond well or if our response clashes with our spouse's response, we can feel the chill of autumn or be thrust into the icy cold of winter—sometimes before we know what hit us.

Some changes, such as sexual infidelity, strike at the very heart of a marriage. Other changes are simply a natural part of life, such as illness, aging, or a new job. Our response to change consists of emotions, attitudes, and actions. The combination of these three factors will determine which season our marriage is in at any given time.

The thesis of this book is that the natural seasons—winter, spring, summer, and fall—provide us with an apt analogy for the changes that occur in our marriage relationships. As we experience life through the five senses—hearing, seeing, smelling, tasting, and touching—we feel emotions, develop attitudes, and take action. The interweaving of our emotions, attitudes, and actions creates the quality of our relationship in the various seasons of marriage.

It has become popular in Western culture over the past forty years to exalt emotions as the guiding light that determines our actions. After more than thirty years of counseling couples, I am convinced this is a misguided notion. Don't misunderstand me: I am not suggesting that emotions are not important. Emotions tell us that something is wrong or right in a relationship, but emotions must lead to reason, and reason must be guided by truth if we are to take constructive action. We must not short-circuit the process and jump straight from emotions to action without the benefit of reason. Many couples who have done this have found themselves in winter when they could have ended up in spring or summer.

EMOTIONS moderated by REASON guided by TRUTH = **CONSTRUCTIVE ACTION**

Let's begin our journey by defining the four seasons of marriage. In the next four chapters, we will look at the common emotions, attitudes, and actions that create a particular season. We will do this by visiting with couples who have chosen to communicate to me the joys and sorrows of their season of marriage. Names and places have been changed to protect the privacy of the couples involved, but the stories are real and for the most part are told in the words of the people themselves.

Perhaps you will discover yourself in one of these seasons of marriage. If not, the Marital Seasons Profile at the end of Part I will help you identify the season of your marriage. In the second part of the book, I will introduce seven practical ideas for weaving your emotions, attitudes, and actions together to move from one season to another.

In Part III, we'll recap the seven strategies and answer some of the common questions I've been asked about the four seasons of marriage.

Finally, to help you use this book in a small-group setting, or to facilitate your own understanding, we've included a study guide intended to promote conversation about the four seasons of marriage and the seven strategies. My hope is that all these features will help you and your spouse enhance the seasons of your marriage.

WINTER

Why begin with winter? I might begin there because that is where the calendar begins, with January. Although it is not true everywhere, January and February in North Carolina are the coldest months. That's when it snows and there are ice storms. It's when people wear gloves and overcoats and when they go sledding in the streets and skiing at Sugar Mountain. Winter is when children look forward to being out of school so they can play in the snow. It is when only the pansies are blooming and the bears are fast asleep. But to be honest, that is not why I want to begin with winter.

I start with winter because most of the people who have been in my counseling office over the past thirty years have come when their marriage was in the season of winter. Not many come to see me when their marriage is enjoying a time of summer. It is the coldness of winter that drives them to my office. In the natural world, at least in North America, we speak of cold winters, harsh winters, snowy winters, icy winters, and bitter winters. In short, winter means difficulty. Life is much harder in the winter than it is in the summer.

Winter marriages are characterized by coldness, harshness, and bitterness. The dreams of spring are covered with layers of ice, and the weather forecast calls for more freezing rain. If the husband and wife have a conversation, it is merely about logistics: who will do what and when. If they try to talk about their relationship, it typically ends in an argument that goes unresolved. Some couples simply live in a cold silence. Essentially, they lead independent lives though they live in the same house. Each spouse blames the other for the coldness of the relationship.

What brings a couple to the winter season of marriage? In a word: *rigidity*—the unwillingness to consider the other person's perspective and to work toward a meaningful compromise. All couples face difficulties, and all couples have differences. These differences may center on money, in-laws, religion, or any other area of life. Couples who fail to negotiate these differences will find themselves in the middle of winter—a season of marriage created not by the difficulties of life but by the manner in which a couple respond to those difficulties. When one or both marriage partners insist on "my way or not at all," they are moving their marriage toward winter.

Winter may last a month, or it may last thirty years. It may begin three months after the wedding or hit in the midlife years. It may focus on one problem area or encompass all of life. As we noted earlier, each season of marriage is accompanied by certain emotions, attitudes, and actions. The interaction of these three factors determines whether a couple will stay in a season or move from one season to another.

In this chapter, I want to describe the emotions, attitudes, and actions that accompany the winter season of marriage. So what does the winter season look like in a marriage?

THE EMOTIONS OF WINTER

Some of the emotions of winter are hurt, anger, and disappointment, often accompanied by loneliness and a sense of rejection.

All the emotions of a couple caught in winter reveal the coldness, harshness, and bitterness that grip the marriage.

Let me introduce you to some couples who are experiencing the winter season of marriage. Listen to the way they describe their emotions:

George is a forty-four-year-old husband from Jacksonville, Florida, who has been married for eighteen years. "My marriage is totally discouraging," he says. "If I were not a Christian, I would probably give up. I know that I should love my wife, but emotionally I am totally empty. It feels as if my wife does not love me, like me, or respect me. It seems that she just tolerates me—and sometimes it doesn't even feel *that* good. I feel terrible about our marriage."

His wife, Helen, describes their marriage this way: "Not fun! Nothing seems to have any flow to it, but I really don't have the emotional energy to get something flowing. My husband has been without a job for a year and a half and apparently is heading in no particular direction. We were in this same position fourteen years ago when he finished graduate school. To have come full circle is extremely frustrating, and to have three children now who have to go through this only adds anxiety. I am very unhappy with the state of our marriage."

Marilyn is forty-five and has been married five years in a second marriage. She says, "I feel disappointed and dejected. We don't talk—only argue—and never come to any conclusions or agreements on how to solve problems. Neither of us is happy. We disagree on money issues and child rearing (my three children live with us). He says that divorce is the only answer. I'm not sure."

Mark has been married for twenty-three years but says of his marriage, "It is very discouraging. We disagree on everything.

11

We are both bullheaded, and this has created many emotional conflicts. There is a coldness about our relationship." His wife, Millie, says, "Mark is very hurtful. We have had many years of resentment. I feel there has been more effort on my part than his. It seems to me that he will not listen and does not care about my feelings. He is *so* critical. At this stage, we spend little time together and give almost no affirmation or touch."

Maria is forty-three and has been married nine years to her second husband. She says of her marriage, "It hurts in so many ways and affects all aspects of my life. I carry it around inside, giving it to the Lord and trying to be optimistic and hopeful. We both want more, but we just can't connect."

Emily has been married for two-and-a-half years but expresses the emotional pain of winter when she says, "I am terribly discontented. It hurts really badly at times. I'm just surviving day by day. I've given up hope."

Hurt, anger, disappointment, loneliness, rejection, and sometimes hopelessness are some of the emotions that couples experience when their marriage is in the season of winter.

THE ATTITUDES OF WINTER

Attitudes are the way we think about or interpret what we experience in life. We frequently speak of people having a negative attitude or a positive attitude. By attitude, I mean the way a person generally responds to the things that happen in life. The winter season of marriage is characterized by negative attitudes.

In winter we tend to see the worst. We perceive problems as too big and positions as too entrenched. We think that disagreements have gone on too long and can never be resolved. We tend to blame our spouse for the decline in our relationship ("If only he would . . ." "If only she wouldn't . . ."). These attitudes foster emotions that range between mild discouragement and utter hopelessness.

I met a man named Frank in Seattle, Washington. He was twenty-four years old and had been married for only a year, but he was extremely distraught about his marriage. "It makes me feel like we are never going to make it. It just keeps getting worse. We fight 24/7, and we hit each other—and we have a baby. I can't go on like this, and I don't know what else to do." In his business, Frank was energetic and always willing to take on new challenges, but at home he was clearly thinking negatively.

After nineteen years of marriage, a woman named Martha said, "I think I really tried to work on our marriage in the early years, but it seemed as if everything I suggested he interpreted as nagging. Nothing seemed to work, so I began to shut down. We've had some times of growth and increased intimacy, but mostly it has centered on what *he* wanted and doesn't involve my needs or desires. That continued pattern has left me not really caring what his needs are at this point. I am now waiting—probably unfairly—for him to put some energy into our marriage."

Here is what Martha's husband, William, said: "A year-and-a-half ago, our marriage had just come off the best two years we'd ever had. We were applying biblical principles to our marriage, and it was great. Martha was trying harder and I lowered my expectations. Then I resigned my job—with her support—but it has been a rough road ever since. Doors have not opened, and I am currently working four part-time jobs to support our family. Apparently, I dropped the ball with communication, consistent affection, and having a plan for the future during the early months of this transition. Since then, Martha has shut down and nothing I do is helping to turn it around. It seems there is a hole

13

in her love tank, and nothing I do gets credited to my account. She says she is not holding on to unforgiveness, but that is what it seems like to me." Clearly Martha and William are both plagued with negative attitudes, and neither is feeling the support of the other.

Sometimes attitudes turn negative quickly. Truett had an offer of another job in a neighboring state. He and Mary discussed it and agreed that this would be a good move for them at this stage in their lives. So they made the move. However, shortly after unpacking, Mary found herself missing her friends and feeling irritated by all the changes that were forced upon her by the move. She complained to Truett about these things and told him how unhappy she was. Truett felt betrayed. He thought they had been in agreement about the move, so he felt that Mary was putting him in an unfair position. He could not resign so soon after accepting his new job, and yet he wanted his wife to be happy.

Mary's negative attitude became a barrier in their marriage, and within a year they were on the brink of divorce. How different things might have been if Mary had taken a positive attitude, sought to make new friends, and looked for the good things in their new situation. Negative attitudes are like a bitter wind that contributes to the winter season of marriage.

THE ACTIONS OF WINTER

Our natural tendency in the middle of winter is to avoid the elements as much as possible. When the weather turns frigid, we retreat inside for survival and wait for it to warm up or for the season to change. In a winter marriage, there may be a similar tendency to "avoid the elements." Spouses may withdraw within themselves, hunkering down and trying to ride out the cold sea-

14

son, hoping for spring but not taking any positive steps to move their marriage toward spring. However, unlike the natural seasons, the seasons of a marriage do not typically change without some positive action—unless it's a change from bad to worse.

If you are experiencing winter in your marriage, your actions will tend to be divisive and destructive. Consciously or subconsciously, they are designed to hurt your spouse. Harsh words, violent acts, or withdrawal and silence are some of the actions of winter. I remember one woman who said to me, "I was so angry because of Kurt's unfaithfulness that I went over to the apartment of the girl I knew he was seeing, found his car, and flattened all four tires with a butcher knife. I know I could have been arrested for that, but at the time I was so angry I just wanted him to know how deeply he was hurting me."

I also remember a husband who told me in the counseling office, "I went over to the apartment where I knew she was living with another man, took the battery out of her car, and threw it in a ditch. I was so angry and hurt."

I met Melody in Racine, Wisconsin, at one of my marriage seminars. At the time, she was in her second marriage; the first marriage had been, in her words, "physically and emotionally abusive." Five years into her second marriage, she was certain that her marriage could be characterized as winter. "I hate it. I am distant, and I don't know if my husband will react positively to anything I initiate. I am tired. I've actually considered telling him we need to separate because I am sure he will never talk civilly to me again. I am not content at all with my marriage at this time." When I asked her to share an example of what was going on in the marriage, she responded, "Two weeks ago, I asked him to stop teasing our son about being a 'momma's boy.' He said I was just playing favorites. Initially, I just walked out of the room, but later that day he said that I was mistreating one of my other sons. It was all downhill after that, and now we are barely speaking. And he avoids me. We are almost never in the same room except to sleep. When he *is* around, I feel he gets verbally abusive. At times, I have memories of my first marriage, and I wonder if the same thing is happening again."

Chris and Amanda attended my seminar in West Palm Beach, Florida. They had been married for five years, and it was the first marriage for both of them. She was twenty-five and he was twenty-nine. Amanda's comments on their marriage indicated that for her it was winter. "I feel sad and hurt, even though at other times it feels like we really love each other. I'm not happy. I want to feel the love we used to feel. We have been through the birth of a child, my husband had a serious accident and was out of work for three years, and our house was destroyed by fire. Over time, we have grown apart. We have become very negative and continue to put each other down."

Chris's comments were brief: "I just know that my wife grew up in a fighting family and doesn't know any other way to live. She is also very demanding." For both Chris and Amanda, critical, demanding, and demeaning words indicated the coldness of their relationship.

Joshua was twenty-two years old and had been married only three years when he said to me, "My wife cheated on me repeatedly with one of my friends in the first six months of our marriage. The way I reacted was by cheating on her. This has caused a lack of trust, among other things, which led us to the winter season. I am definitely not content with our marriage. I've made many bad decisions before, and I worry about making things worse."

Bernice is seventy-eight years old and has been married fifty-four years to the same husband, but she admits that her marriage is very painful. "I feel rejected and discouraged," she said. "My husband is a recovering alcoholic and is often depressed. He lies to me or he doesn't talk to me at all, and lately he's been getting into pornography. My heart is broken, but all I know to do is pray. If I try to talk with him, he is critical and blames me for all our problems. Yes, our marriage is definitely in the winter season. It's really sad after all these years together."

In the winter season of marriage, communication fluctuates between silence and arguments. Critical words are spoken that further hurt the relationship. Verbal abuse sometimes leads to physical abuse. The sexual part of the marriage becomes a battlefield, and sexual unfaithfulness may strike the final blow to the marriage.

A winter marriage is indeed cold, harsh, and bitter. Eventually, couples become detached emotionally and sometimes physically. They may sleep in separate bedrooms because they do not want to be close to each other. Sexually and emotionally, they are already divorced. If the warm winds of spring do not come soon, they may take steps to become legally divorced as well.

Winter is often accompanied by feelings of desperation. Bryan, who was in his midtwenties and had been married for four years, said of his marriage, "We were obsessed with each other in the beginning. Now we are confused. I am trying to accept her, but just this morning she said that the devil had a foothold in her life. I want to help, but I don't know what to do. I am not content with our relationship. Communication is one sided: from her to me. When I do speak up, she finishes my sentences, so mostly I keep quiet. But I am afraid of how far this might go. I don't push my opinions. I let her rule and don't understand why."

Bryan's wife, Christy, said, "We allowed Satan a foothold in our lives by engaging in premarital sex. Now we are married but I resent his touch, and there is a bitterness and anger that I realize only God can heal. I hope it comes soon."

Marge is forty-five and has been married eight years to her second husband. "I don't understand why or how it got this way, but our marriage is just an existence. We let the kids—two of his, two of mine—rip us apart in our early years. The kids are grown and gone now (all but one), but we are struggling to put our lives back together. I don't know how to fix our marriage."

Typically, marriages do not begin in the winter season. And unlike the natural seasons, fall does not always precede winter in a marriage. A marriage can move directly from spring to winter. For Joanie, it seemed that her marriage went straight from the honeymoon to winter. It was her second marriage, and she had a mentally challenged child from her first marriage. "While we were dating, Jon seemed to like Mandy. He was always kind to her. But after the honeymoon, it was like Mandy was suddenly a bother to him. He wanted it to be just the two of us. Well, that's not a possibility. He's living in a fantasy world. He even asked me if we could find someone to adopt Mandy. Why would I want to do that? She's my daughter. I think I made a huge mistake in marrying Jon. I don't know if we can ever get it together. He loses his temper, and his words destroy me. He has to call all the shots in our lives. It's like my opinions don't matter to him."

Winter may come early in a marriage or it may come after fifty years. In between, it can occur many times. Couples can recognize it by their emotions, their attitudes, and their actions. The chart on page 19 summarizes the basic signs of a winter marriage.

THE POSITIVE SIDE OF WINTER

If your marriage is in winter, it may appear beyond hope. But don't give up. Just as most people wouldn't lie down in the snow

WINTER	
EMOTIONS:	Hurt, anger, disappointment, loneliness, feeling rejected
ATTITUDES:	Negativity, discouragement, frustration, hopelessness
ACTIONS:	Destructive, speaking harshly, not speaking, violent
CLIMATE OF RELATIONSHIP:	Detached, cold, harsh, bitter. In the winter season of marriage, couples are unwilling to negotiate differences. Conversations turn to arguments, or spouses withdraw in silence. There is no sense of togetherness. The marriage is like two people living in separate igloos.

and wait to die, there's no reason to passively accept the coldness of a wintry marriage. There is a way out, and it begins with hope. The coldness of winter often stimulates a desire for healing and health. It is the sick who seek a physician and find healing. A winter marriage often makes couples desperate enough to break out of their silent suffering and seek the help of a counselor, pastor, or trusted friend. Those who seek help will find it.

Through the process of healing, couples come to experience the positive side of winter. As one husband said, "We realized that through the pain we rediscovered our roots, affirmed our faith, and grew in character." Often it is the trials of life that produce patience and perseverance.[1] God can use marital winters for good.[2] Working through the season of winter may never be "fun" or "exciting," like sledding down a steep hill or a ski trip to Vail, but when couples persevere and begin to take positive steps to improve their marriage, they emerge stronger, more committed, and better able to work through their differences.

Through the years, I have seen numerous couples move from

winter to spring. When the failures of winter are confessed and forgiven, forgiveness makes room for love, and "love covers over a multitude of sins."³ By extending the olive branch of peace, even in the midst of pain and alienation, countless couples have discovered the potential for deep healing and an even deeper intimacy. The scars of failure are reminders of sin, a desperate need for forgiveness, and the power of God to save. The good news is that forgiveness and God's power are always available to those who seek them. When two people choose to love again, the melting ice of winter will water the seeds of spring, and winter has served its ultimate purpose.

In Part II, we will look at the tools necessary to move from winter to spring. But first, let's identify the characteristics of the other three seasons of marriage.

SPRING

In the world of nature, spring is the time for new beginnings. In my corner of the world, I know it is spring when the crocuses lift their heads above the soil and smile. They are soon followed by the daffodils and the greening of the grass. On occasions when the crocuses celebrate too early, I've seen them blanketed with snow, but this never seems to bother them. It is as if they know that winter's last fling will soon give way to the reign of spring. Inspired by the courage of the crocuses, all nature begins to bud and soon blossoms into its full beauty. As it happens, the arrival of spring often intersects with Easter, which celebrates the ultimate triumph of life over death.

Spring is where most marriages begin, the excitement of creating a new life together giving men and women the courage to make a covenant marriage commitment. "To love and to cherish, in sickness and in health, in poverty and in wealth, so long as we both shall live." These words have the ring of spring. What could be more exciting than joining two lives together to help each other accomplish the purposes for which they were created? Yes, marriages begin in the springtime.

Janet, a thirty-three-year-old newlywed I met at a marriage seminar in Alabama, captured the excitement of spring when she described her six-month-old marriage: "It's full of joy! It's exciting to watch our relationship grow and develop. That 'in love' high just deepens and becomes richer each day. Every day is an opportunity to find a way to live out my love for my husband. In some ways, it's scary because there is that fear of not measuring up. And having older couples express their thoughts of 'just wait a few years and it won't be so wonderful' makes me think, *Why not? Can't we make the daily choice to keep this joy alive and maturing?*" Janet was excited and happy about her marriage, and she intended to keep it that way. She was a bit ruffled by people who would want to snow on her crocuses, but she was certain that their dire predictions need not become a reality.

Marriage is not a lifelong springtime, but we can come back to the optimism, enthusiasm, and joy of spring many times in the course of our lives. We'll inevitably have our seasons of summer, fall, and winter as well, though not necessarily in that predictable order. As mentioned earlier, the seasons of marriage are not chronological, and thus springtime is not exclusively for newlyweds. The seasons repeat themselves numerous times throughout a marriage, and because we are creatures of choice, we can create new beginnings whenever we desire. More about the process later, but first let's visit with some couples who are in the springtime of marriage.

As we've seen, the seasons of a marriage are created by the changes we encounter and—more important—by our emotions, attitudes, and actions. Emotions typically influence our attitudes and our actions. For example, if I feel angry, the anger can develop into an attitude and I act it out. Conversely, the emotion of joy may lead to an attitude of optimism, which in turn results in the action of encouraging others. When couples describe their emotions, attitudes, and actions, they are describing the quality of their marriage relationships, or the season of their marriage. So, what does a springtime marriage look like?

THE EMOTIONS OF SPRING

Spring is characterized by animated and buoyant feelings, such as excitement, joy, hope, and happiness.

Amanda from Little Rock, Arkansas, is thirty-three and has been married for a year. "It's exciting," she says. "We've been together for ten years of dating, but marriage brings a whole new aspect to our relationship. Now I have a husband whom I love, and I know he loves me. It's new; I see him in a different light. I'm excited about what the future holds for us."

Brandon got married for the first time at age forty-five. He's been married for two years and says, "I'm excited about our marriage as we continue our journey together. It's been a little scary as we have tried to take our emotions to a deeper level by learning each other's love language. I am really happy to be married to a woman who wants to continue growing and not let our relationship become stale. I want to keep on learning how to be a better husband."

23

I met Joyce and Rob at one of my marriage seminars in Tampa, Florida. At one of the breaks, after we had chatted a bit, I asked Joyce to describe her marriage in terms of one of the four seasons. She said, "After listening to the first half of your seminar, I feel very blessed to be in the spring season of our marriage. Our excitement over being married has subsided slightly, but I still get that excited feeling at times when I look at my husband. Yes, I am happier now than I have ever been in my life! I love my husband and I love being married."

"How long have you been married?" I asked.

"Seven years."

Rex and Bonnie have been married for twenty-six years and live in Richmond, Virginia. Rex said, "Our first child was born the day after our first anniversary, so it seems like we have always had kids at home. Now we are empty nesters and have only each other. We find we are enjoying our time together—our conversations and our sharing of thoughts, concerns, and interests. We enjoy doing things together. Our grown kids say they want to find marriage relationships like their parents enjoy. That is very gratifying to both of us." After twenty-six years, Rex and Bonnie are rediscovering the springtime of marriage.

I met Ryan and Michelle in Phoenix, Arizona. "We are entering a new stage of our marriage," Ryan said. "It's like we are starting all over again. We moved here three years ago from the Midwest, and it has been like a second honeymoon for us. Before we moved, we were beginning to get into a rut and, frankly, not giving much attention to each other. Since the move, we have spent a lot more time talking with each other and doing things together. Both of us have found a new excitement about life and about our marriage. We are the happiest we have ever been."

On another occasion, after I had completed a lecture titled "Making Sex a Mutual Joy," a woman named Leslie said to me, "It's true. I love being married to Sean—and besides all that, our sex life is terrific! It's like I have rediscovered my femininity, and I feel so loved by my husband. It's a whole new season in our marriage." Sean and Leslie were experiencing the emotions of spring.

THE ATTITUDES OF SPRING

In the springtime of marriage, spouses have positive attitudes toward each other and toward life in general. The typical attitudes of spring are gratitude and anticipation of the future. Change is perceived as an opportunity for new beginnings, and springtime couples fully expect to make the best of those opportunities. We sometimes speak of the pessimist as a person who sees a glass half empty, whereas the optimist sees it half full. A pessimist says, "It looks like it's going to rain." An optimist says, "We may get a sprinkle, but I think it's going to be a beautiful day." In the season of spring, couples have an optimistic attitude about their marriages.

In the world of nature, spring has its pollen. If people curse the pollen, you know that spring is not their favorite time of the year. But if they talk optimistically about the flowers and the butterflies (even while sneezing from the pollen), you know that they are in love with spring. The same is true in a marriage. Even in the springtime, there can be difficulties, but the prevailing attitude is one of anticipated growth rather than despair. Jill, from upstate New York, described the attitude of spring well when she said, "I feel that our marriage is growing. Of course, we have our ups and downs like anyone else. But we are trying to build our lives around the teachings of Christ. We are learning to communicate, learning how to nurture our love, and learning how to be open to each other's ideas and feelings. We are excited about being together and exploring the future with God."

Not only is springtime characterized by an attitude of optimism, it is also accompanied by an attitude of gratitude. Joanie had been married to Alex for twenty-two years when she said to me, "Things aren't where I want them to be, but I am hopeful for the future. I'm grateful for what I have, and I want us to keep growing. When I see other marriages falling apart, I'm glad that Alex and I still love each other and are continuing to work at our relationship."

Alex expressed a similar attitude: "We've learned to communicate pretty well. We've learned that we don't have to agree on everything. Sometimes we agree to disagree and seek to understand each other's point of view. But we love each other and that is the central focus, along with our love for God. That helps us overcome any differences we have, because we agree more than we disagree. I'm deeply grateful for the marriage God has given us."

The attitude of love blossoms beautifully in the spring. As Janet from Alabama said after six months of marriage, "Every day is an opportunity to find a way to live out my love for my husband." She is expressing an attitude of love.

Amy, a woman I met in Indianapolis, said, "My husband is very considerate, and that has rubbed off on me. We both are very aware of each other's feelings and try to make a conscious effort to nurture our relationship. We love each other, and we want to keep it alive forever."

If it is springtime in your marriage, you will be consciously thinking about things you might do or say to express your love to your mate. Last Sunday, after the morning worship service at our church, I was greeted by a couple who have been married for thirty-five years. The husband said, "Last week we took a vacation, and we took your book *The Five Love Languages: Men's Edition* with us. I read your original book several years ago, and I thought I understood my wife's love language. But this week we both learned a lot about each other. It's been one of the best weeks we've had in years. We feel like we are beginning a second honeymoon, only this time our love is so much deeper than it was in the early years of our marriage." It was obvious to me that spring had returned after thirty-five years of marriage.

Springtime is also undergirded by an attitude of trust. Trust is believing that your spouse is a person of integrity—that he or she will tell you the truth. If your marriage is built on a solid foundation of trust, you are certain of your spouse's faithfulness to the marital commitment, and you will choose to believe the best about your mate, even in uncertain circumstances. The attitude of trust brings a sense of security. I've never forgotten what one young man said to me a few years ago: "We've been married ten years, and one of the greatest things for me is the trust that I have in Misty. My father could not trust my mother; she had numerous involvements with other men through the years. It was a great source of grief for my father, although I always admired the fact that he forgave her and sought to recover. Mom died six years ago, and Dad is now married to a wonderful Christian woman. I'm really happy for him. I guess because of all that, I am so grateful for Misty and her love and commitment to me. Knowing that I can trust her brings me great joy." He was expressing one of the characteristic attitudes of spring.

When we foster the springtime attitudes of optimism, gratitude, love, and trust, we will enjoy the fragrant blossoming of spring in our marriages. Such attitudes lead to positive actions.

THE ACTIONS OF SPRING

For most of us, spring brings us out of the house into a whole new world of activity. Who doesn't enjoy a spring picnic, ants and all? In many parts of the country, spring means mowing the grass and planting the garden. On top of that is the whole world of spring sports that provide recreation for the kids and turn Mom into a taxi service. Spring is a time for accelerated activity, and most of us are happy to emerge from our winter dens and participate in the excitement.

Similarly, when spring comes to a marriage relationship, it will be characterized by new attitudes and new activities. We look for ways to express our love and stimulate excitement in our relationship. These are not random actions—activity for activity's sake—nor are they self-centered. The focus is on bringing new life to the marriage and building up the good that is already there. In this season of marriage, the guiding principle is *nurture*, which means "to feed." The actions of springtime are designed to feed and nourish the marital relationship. Both spouses seek to do things that will enhance the life of their mate. They ask themselves, "How will this affect our relationship?" If a marriage is in the season of spring, both spouses will do things to deepen the relationship and benefit the other person.

Ashley had been married for seven years and spoke excitedly when she said to me, "We have finally established date nights, to talk or do whatever we want. I am now okay with leaving our children with grandparents." This "fresh start" action—establishing a new habit of date nights—indicates that Ashley and her husband, Grey, are moving into spring.

Heidi and Jeremy have been married one year. "We're newlyweds!" Heidi said. "We are reading books on communication and marriage. We are attending conferences about how to keep our marriage healthy, and we are asking God to lead us in our lives and be a part of our marriage. We are both very fortunate to have come from Christian homes, and we both grew up with wonderful models. We are excited about the future." Heidi and Jeremy are not resting on the laurels of their parents but taking positive action to see that their marriage stays "on track."

In the first two-and-a-half years of their marriage, Jake and Kendra had already experienced a season of winter. But when I met them, they were definitely experiencing spring. "How did you make the transition?" I asked.

"I eliminated my part-time job," Jake replied. "We had realized that we simply did not have time to work on our marriage. The money was nice but it wasn't worth it. We made a move to another town only thirty miles away and it gave us a fresh start. We both rekindled our individual relationships with God. This has made a big difference."

Kendra added, "When we brought God back into our lives, we began to see the positive things about each other and focused on those. We began to pray together and play together. It has made a world of difference for us. We are actually enjoying being married again. We know that God has good things for us in the future."

I met Julian and Dorothy in Richmond, Virginia. Julian opened the conversation by saying, "We want to tell you how much we appreciate your writing. It has opened to us a whole new world of understanding each other."

"For twenty-five years," Dorothy said, "I wondered what made him tick. Then I discovered that his love languages are quality time and physical touch. My love languages are words of affirmation and acts of service. When I stopped cleaning, cooking, and painting; took time to sit down and talk with him face-to-face; and started giving him loving touches, he began doing acts of service and giving me words of affirmation. We have entered a whole new stage of marriage."

"It's called springtime," I said. "And I hope you stay there a long time."

Obviously, making positive changes requires a willingness to change. Madelyn was twenty-one and had been married for only ten months when I met her and her husband, Jackson, in Sumter, South Carolina. "We got off to a rough start in our marriage," she said, "but God has worked positively in our lives to get us over the hump. He revealed to us our own selfishness.

We still have disagreements occasionally, but I am continually humbled and disarmed by my husband's willingness to look at what he is doing and be open to change. That makes me love him more and more."

Jackson added, "We have only begun this season with God's help and understanding. We took a class on marriage at our church and realized that we are both incomplete people and God has a desire to see us changed. He is using our marriage to help both of us grow." I predict that if Madelyn and Jackson continue with their willingness to change, they will live in the springtime or summer most of their lives. Loving actions, which begin with a willingness to change, create a positive emotional climate between a husband and wife that makes life exciting.

Positive actions require time. Dave, from Atlanta, has been married twenty-one years and has three children. "One of the things that has kept our marriage alive and growing is that we chiseled time into our schedules to spend together doing things we mutually enjoy. We have experienced tragedies in our family, and that has forced us to realize the importance of nurturing our marriage." I like the picture that Dave used—"we chiseled time into our schedules." If we don't make time for each other, no one else will do it for us.

Learning how to take positive action sometimes requires outside help. For Jerry and Jan, the first eight years of marriage were, in a word, *miserable*. "We didn't agree on anything," Jan said. "We spent most of our time arguing, and both of us had come to regret that we had married. But all that changed a year ago. We've taken steps, both together and individually, through Christian counseling. We've learned to accept responsibility for ourselves and to enjoy the uniqueness of each other without controlling the other. The one key element for us is having Christ in our lives and learning to be more like him." Jerry and Jan illustrate the reality that some couples will need professional help. Being willing to go for counseling is a positive action that often results in the return of spring.

Andrew and Tricia got off to a much healthier start. When I met them two years into their marriage, Andrew said, "Before we got married, we sought out mentors and wise, trusted counselors to help us prepare for our life together. Communication has been a big part of our relationship. Before marriage, we communicated expectations and how families play into our lives and marriage. One of the things we learned was to laugh together every day. There is something about laughter that makes life easier. We seek at least one way every day to express our love to each other: notes, actions, or words. We've had a great two years and anticipate a great future."

Positive attitudes engender positive actions. And loving actions result in positive emotions. Wrap these three together and you have the springtime of marriage. In summary, a spring marriage looks like this:

SPRING	
EMOTIONS:	Excitement, joy, hope
ATTITUDES:	Anticipation, optimism, gratitude, love, trust
ACTIONS:	Nurturing, planning, communicating, seeking help when needed
CLIMATE OF RELATIONSHIP:	Vital, tender, open, caring. Spring is a time of new beginnings. The flowers are blooming. The streams of communication are flowing. There is a sense of excitement about life together. Couples are making plans. They have great hopes for the future. They are planting seeds from which they hope to reap a harvest of happiness.

THE DOWNSIDE OF SPRING

Lest you think that spring has no problems, let me warn you about poison ivy. A few years ago, as I was getting ready to plant my spring garden, I learned an important lesson in plant identification. The season before, I had erected a wire fence to protect my garden from rabbits. As I was turning the soil, preparing it for planting, I noticed ivy growing on my fence. *Where did that come from?* I thought. *I didn't plant any ivy.* With a few fast pulls of the hand, I removed the ivy from my fence. The next day, when I woke up with itching welts on my hand and wrist, I realized I had tangled with *poison* ivy. For the next few days, I was greatly irritated by intense itching.

In a springtime marriage, we may encounter poison ivy—irritations that pop up unannounced and unexpected. These irritations can cause marital itching, even in the midst of springtime. They can ruin a perfectly wonderful vacation or turn a fine dinner into an emotional fiasco. These irritations do not change the season, but they may make spring less enjoyable. As part of Strategy 6, we will discuss how to turn these irritations into assets as we "maximize" our differences. For the moment, however, let me encourage you to share your irritations with your spouse and be open to change.

Spring often leads a couple to make positive changes. It is a time of new beginnings, new patterns of life, new ways of listening and expressing concern, and new ways of loving. If we successfully implement and nurture these positive changes, springtime will give way to the fun and warmth of summer. On the other hand, if we fail to follow through with new beginnings, we may find ourselves skipping summer altogether and slipping straight into fall or winter. But missing summer is like missing the ice-cream truck. It's enough to make a grown man cry. In the next chapter, we will look at the season of marriage that you don't want to miss.

SUMMER

Beyond the elm tree, closer to the creek, I planted five crape myrtles. The first few years they grew slowly—maybe because of poor soil or my lack of attention. But this summer they are in full bloom, heavy laden with clusters of red. I have learned from others that crape myrtles bloom at different times, even in the same geographical location. Up by the apartment complex on the highway, they started blooming in early June, but the ones I planted bloom in mid-to-late July. They signal for me that summer reigns.

At this time of year, we are also eating fresh corn, okra, and tomatoes. Nothing tastes better than a vine-ripened tomato in the middle of summer. I have some friends who would say the same thing about watermelon or squash. Summer is when the gardener reaps the benefits of what was planted and nurtured in the spring.

For children, summer is the time to relax. School is closed and the pool is open. And if one lives near a creek, as I do, it's fun to catch tadpoles. The sun stays awake longer and so do the kids. Hot, sweaty faces indicate intense activity, but for children, it is sheer joy. "Do we have to come inside? We're having fun" is the mantra of summer.

Fun is also the theme of a summer marriage. Life is beautiful. We are reaping the benefits of our hard efforts to understand each other and to work together as a team to see the dreams of spring fulfilled. The anticipation of spring has turned into the reality of summer. The initial excitement may have waned, but our sense of connection with each other has deepened. We have fewer misunderstandings, and when we do, resolutions come more quickly.

We may or may not have reached our financial goals. We may or may not have children. We may have good health or poor health. Our vocation may be satisfying or frustrating. But if our marriage is in the season of summer, we will share a deep sense of commitment and satisfaction. And we will feel secure in each other's love.

So what are the emotions, attitudes, and actions that foster and sustain the season of summer in a marriage? From Maine to Miami and from Seattle to San Diego, I've encountered couples who have described their marriage as being in the summer season. Let's look at a few examples.

THE EMOTIONS OF SUMMER

Summer is characterized by feelings of happiness, satisfaction, accomplishment, and connection. Look for the words that describe these emotions in the following stories:

Julia is thirty-seven years old and has been married for sixteen years. "Summer feels good," she said. "We're on the 'same page,' and as my husband always says, it 'makes our marriage fun.' It opens up my heart to communication."

Hal is sixty-three and has been married to Geneva for forty-one years. I met them in Pasadena, California. He said, "It is a good feeling to be content with myself and my wife in this season of life. By content, I do not mean that I have stopped working to make it better. I just mean that there is something there that I can't put into words, but I just know that things are right between the two of us. We are there for each other." As Hal smiled at Geneva, she nodded and added, "That's right. And we intend to keep it that way."

I met Marc at one of my marriage seminars in Spokane, Washington. He had been married to Jennifer for twenty years. He said, "I feel that we are in the summer of our marriage. In the past we have been overwhelmed with issues, including work, raising children, and a lot of physical problems. But we worked our way through those and are stronger because of them. Our relationship seems comfortable. There's no longer the struggle of those earlier years. It's a good feeling to know that we have survived and really do love each other." Marc is a quiet, reserved man, and I could tell that his words expressed the deep sense of satisfaction that he felt inside. Jennifer added, "I'm so glad we didn't give up when things were tough. What we have now was worth working for."

Marsha is twenty-nine and has been married ten months. She and Reg live in Tampa, Florida. When I asked her to describe her marriage, she said, "It feels good now—much better than the first eight-and-a-half months." Looking at Reg, she added, "He finally understands what I meant when I said, 'I don't feel special. I don't feel like you love me. You don't do things like you did before we got married.' When he discovered my love language and started speaking it, I felt loved again. The last two months have definitely been summer for me."

"What about you, Reg?" I inquired.

"She's speaking my love language. I feel good about our relationship," he said. "Marsha's pregnant with our first baby. I just hope we can keep summer alive after the baby comes." Obviously,

35

Reg and Marsha were feeling connected again after getting off to a rocky start in their marriage.

Summer may come at a busy time of life, but the busyness need not destroy the intimacy. Tricia is twenty-four and has been married to Rob for three years. They live in Tucson, Arizona. She said, "I feel comfortable with our relationship. Although we are very busy with our jobs, we still are happy and able to spend quality time together. I think we both feel secure in each other's love, and I hope we can keep it this way forever."

Celeste lives in Arlington, Texas, and has been married to Daniel for fourteen years. It is her second marriage, his first. She said, "Our marriage is definitely in the summer season. It gives me a feeling of peace and confidence to know that I can trust Daniel. He is so caring, and I hope that he knows I love him more than anyone in the world." She reached out and held Daniel's hand. He smiled and said, "I really believe that. And I love her more than anyone in the world. We are so happy that God has given us a good marriage." *Happiness, satisfaction, peace, fun, comfort*—these are words that describe the emotions of a couple who are living in the summer season of marriage.

THE ATTITUDES OF SUMMER

Our deck is filled with beautiful potted flowers: impatiens, Gerber daisies, hibiscus, petunias, geraniums, and portulaca. They have been blooming profusely all summer long. However, one observation I have made is that if flowers are not watered, they wilt. The first to drop their heads when the water ceases to flow are the impatiens. Perhaps that is where they got their name.

Summer marriages are much like flowers: They are beautiful, but they must be watered. Couples who are successful at having an extended season of summer in their marriage are ones who have learned to maintain what they have attained. They recognize that the summer season did not come without preparing the soil, planting the seeds, and nurturing the marriage. Now that they are enjoying the beauty of summer, they want to maintain it, and they have an attitude of work and growth. Almost without exception, couples who tell me that their marriage is in the summer season also say that they have a desire to continue growing.

I met Candace in Auburn, Alabama. She had been married five years to Tim, and they were definitely in the summer season of marriage. She said, "It feels like living with my best friend. It's fun and I really enjoy it. But I realize that we must continue to nurture the romantic part of our relationship. Otherwise, the busyness will push us apart."

Tim echoed this attitude about growth when he said, "I see summer as slightly more mature than spring. Some of the fantasy has faded, and we are learning that love, affection, romance, and time together can still happen—and should happen—in spite of the daily routine. *Comfortable* is really a good word for it. We know each other well enough that we have seen plenty of faults, but we love each other anyway. And we are still growing stronger and more in love all the time. We've seen that life can be hard, but it has drawn us closer, both to each other and to God. We know that love is a daily thing, and our intention is to keep it alive."

Max and Brenda, from Columbus, Ohio, have been married for twelve years. They describe their marriage as being in the summer season, and it is obvious that their attitude is one of growth. Max says, "I am happy to be in the summer season of my marriage. We feel comfortable with each other, but I know we cannot simply drift through this season. We know each other well, and we must continue to seek out each other and not simply get into a rut. I want us to continue exploring new opportunities, traveling to new places, and generally communicating our love to each other."

Brenda's comments reflected the same attitude: "We are content with our lives, jobs, raising our son, church, and many other things. We enjoy each other and are able to work through conflicts quicker than earlier in our marriage. We are more purposeful in caring for each other than we were five or six years ago. I want us to continue working on our marriage, because I know that things can be even better if we continue to communicate and think about how we can serve each other."

Amanda had experienced a difficult life. She was in her third marriage and had been married for two years. She said, "It's very satisfying to be in the summer season of our marriage. I am happy in this state, but I know that there is always room for improvement. I brought five children into this marriage, and my husband had never been married and has no children. So we have had many major adjustments. But God has been so faithful. I'm looking forward to continued growth. I'm just glad that my husband is willing to listen and work with me as we blend our lives together."

Summer does not equal perfection, but it does mean that couples in this season have a sense of accomplishment and a desire to keep growing. Most couples in the summer season of marriage realize that it took work to get there. They have a positive attitude about their marriage, they are enjoying their spouse, and they intend to continue "watering the flowers." These attitudes lead to positive actions that keep the summer happiness flowing.

THE ACTIONS OF SUMMER

For most of us, summer is a time of increased activity. We travel to new places and have new experiences. Or we make our annual pilgrimage to the beach house or the mountains, where we relive the experiences of past summers and make new memories for the future. Summer does not create activities, but it provides a climate in which they can flourish. Typically, children are out of school, we have a couple weeks of vacation accrued at work, and the weather invites us to enjoy nature. Most families are responsive to this invitation, and summer is a busy but fun season.

In a summer marriage, the warm emotional climate fosters positive actions. The atmosphere is relaxed. We understand our spouse better, we accept each other's differences, and we have learned how to resolve our conflicts. Though life is comfortable, we still want to take some positive actions to "water the flowers" in our summer marriage.

Constructive Communication

Constructive communication is an important component of a summer marriage. I first met Nancy in Bangor, Maine. She was forty-eight and had been married for six years. She indicated that her marriage was definitely in the summer season. "I enjoy being married. I married for the first time at the age of forty-two. I was a happy single person, and I like being married." When I asked what she considered to be the most important thing in their relationship, she answered with one word, "Talk!"

"That's it," she said. "My husband brought a twelve-year-old son and fourteen-year-old daughter into our marriage. We had to talk or we could not have handled the teen years and a drug-addicted, alcoholic ex-wife who rejected her children. I never imagined that the children would not want everything to work out as much as I did. My husband and I had to talk a lot to each other, and we had to talk a lot with the children. Talking has given us a good marriage, and I hope we never stop."

Over and over again, as I interviewed couples who considered their marriages to be in the summer season, they emphasized open communication. Jeremy and Ruth got married at eighteen and have been married for thirty years. They live in St. Louis, Missouri. Ruth described their marriage as definitely in a summer season. "We have been best friends since before we married and are still best friends today—which makes our marriage fun, comfortable, connected, and happy. Because we have gone through some real problems over the last few years, we have had to talk even more. We both enjoy talking, which is great when you have been married thirty years. It feels very secure and very reassuring to be in the summer season of our marriage."

"So what created such a super marriage?" I asked.

"When we married, we had the traditional vows, but privately we had some 'extra' vows that we try to live by. One, an open-door policy, no matter what. That is, we agreed that if anything was bothering one of us, the other wanted to be approached and would be willing to talk about it. Two, we never let the sun go down on our anger. We knew that anger could be destructive to a marriage if not resolved. Incidentally, we've spent many a night up till the wee hours of the morning," she said with a smile. "Number three, we each take care of our appropriate family members in the way we see fit, because we were both raised so differently." These, to Ruth, were the keys to "watering the flowers" of summer.

In my counseling practice, I have observed over the years that couples who have open communication also come to practical solutions, such as the one that Ruth and Jeremy discovered about dealing with potential in-law problems. When couples communicate openly with each other, they are far more likely to find workable solutions to what could otherwise be serious problems in their marriage.

Jeremy's description of his marriage was very similar to Ruth's. "It's very refreshing to be in a marriage that has weathered a variety of seasons, to know that the investment you have made in someone's life is paying dividends, not only in our relationship but with our families and children."

"How did you create this summer season?" I asked.

"Simple," he replied. "We decided up front to be open and honest with each other, to never go to bed mad or harbor anger or resentment. We agreed to forgive, forget, and move forward in the love we have that is founded on the love of Christ." It was obvious to me that Jeremy and Ruth knew one of the secrets to continuing to live in the summer season of marriage. Why is communication so important? Because it is the process by which spouses get to know each other and learn to work together as a team.

It is not always easy to make time for communication, but it is always possible. Jeanette and Sam have been married for twenty-seven years. "I am very content in my marriage," she said. "We are looking forward to my husband's retiring from his present job and going into full-time ministry. We have had many good times, but we have also had many very hard times. But we both seek to find ways to encourage each other. The key to our marriage, as I see it, is that we have tried to spend time just talking. Sometimes we will take a walk; other times we will take a car ride so we can be alone to talk. We have five children, and my in-laws live with us. My daughter and her husband also live with us at the moment, but they have bought a house and will be moving out in a couple of months. Most of the time, we have to get out of the house so we can talk. Sometimes we have short conversations when he comes home from work. He finds me, wherever I am, and we talk about how the day has gone. It's that short communication time that keeps us feeling connected."

Acceptance of Differences

A second important action to maintain a summer marriage is granting each other the freedom to be different. Differences are inevitable, but they can also be very divisive. Couples who desire to continue in the summer season will consciously give each other the freedom to think, feel, and react differently.

Lauren and Dean have been married for eight years. It is a second marriage for both of them. They both agreed that one of the things that has kept their marriage in the summer season is a positive attitude about differences. "We accept each other's differences," Dean noted. "This has been and will continue to be a learning and growing process for us. Both of us learned from our previous marriages that if couples don't accept differences, they will spend the bulk of their time fighting. We agreed that we would rather be lovers than fighters, so we give each other the freedom to be different."

I met Vivian in Jefferson City, Missouri. She was seventy-four years old and had been married for fifty-three years. "I feel very blessed to have a great marriage. We have our little ups and downs, but we love each other so much and feel so blessed to have each other. We have learned to overlook our shortcomings and focus on the positive things. We both feel that life is precious, and with the Lord's help we will make it together. We share our hurts and our joys. Recently, we experienced the tragic death of our son. But God is with us, and we are with each other. So we will make it." Learning to overlook your spouse's shortcomings is a key to keeping the flowers of a summer marriage blooming.

Seminars and Books

A third action step that is common among couples who describe their marriage as being in the summer season is attending marriage seminars and reading books on marriage. When I met Gary and Barb from Roanoke, Virginia, they had been married for twenty-eight years and were definitely in the summer season of marriage. Barb said, "I am content in knowing that my husband loves me and I love him. We have had trying times recently with our daughter's divorce, as she and our granddaughter have come to live with us. But our love and marriage have only grown stronger. The thing that I think has helped us the most is attending marriage seminars. Each year for the past seven years, we have attended the fall Festival of Marriage sponsored by LifeWay Christian Resources.[1] It has helped us tremendously. And, of course, what we are learning today from you simply adds to that. I would encourage couples to attend a marriage seminar every year."

Samantha and Andrew have been married seventeen years and live in Colorado Springs. Samantha describes her marriage as "summer with a bit of fall." She said, "We've had some tough years. But about three years ago we took a class called His Needs, Her Needs at our church. Between that class and studying the book *The Five Love Languages,* I realized that by seeking to meet Andrew's needs and keeping his love tank full, I make it easier for him to meet my needs. But it took me fourteen years to get to that point. And even now, if I am not willing to communicate my thoughts and feelings, things begin to fall apart. I know we need to keep learning. We've decided that from this point on, we're going to attend a marriage conference every year." I especially like the comment that Samantha made as she walked away: "My mind-set for life has been that I would rather attempt to do something and fail than to do nothing and succeed."

With that attitude and with their plans for positive action,

Samantha and Andrew, I predict, will spend more of their time enjoying the flowers of summer in their marriage.

Spiritual Growth

Many couples have indicated to me that the most significant factor in their ability to have a summer marriage is that they have found ways to stimulate spiritual growth. Bekah and Jon have been married for nine years. She said, "It feels great to have confidence in someone who you know has the same goal you do in marriage. We have not always been in the summer season, but when we gave our marriage to God and allowed him to work, things changed dramatically. We now know there is a greater purpose for us than having a great marriage, and that is to bring glory to God. It has brought an added dimension to our lives and our marriage."

Van and Maria live in Auburn, Alabama, and have been married for fourteen years. Van said, "We are deeply religious, and we account most of the success of our marriage to that. The church has kept us connected as a couple. We have participated in small groups, both as a couple and as individuals. This has really helped keep us accountable. There is something about being involved with other Christians that stimulates positive actions between the two of us. I can't say enough about how God has used our church in our lives. Maria and I pray together. We both read the Bible individually and share with each other things we've read. We read Christian books together and we talk openly almost every day. We seek to do little things for each other that will enrich our lives. God has given us a genuine love for each other. I wouldn't exchange it for anything."

Because God instituted marriage, it makes sense that couples who seek to learn from him would have the best possible marriages. Research indicates that this is true.[2]

STAYING IN SUMMER

Every marriage will have its summer seasons, but how can couples *keep* their marriage in summer? To answer this question, I'd like to introduce you to two couples—one couple who have been married a short time, the other for longer. Notice the various elements of summer that they weave into their descriptions of their marriages and how they maintain them.

Mick and Lucy live in Augusta, Georgia. Mick said, "We dated for nearly four years before we married. We've been married now for five years. In those years, we have been through a lot: moving across the country, searching for a new job, my parents' divorcing after nearly thirty years of marriage, and many other things. These struggles helped to ground us in our own marriage. Through prayer, Bible study, our love for each other, and the support of Christian friends and family, we have worked our way through these challenges. We have a 'date night' once a week, even if it's just sitting on the couch together, taking a walk, or going out for ice cream. No matter what, we make sure we show each other our love daily. We realize that as a couple we have to work on our marriage, and it's actually a lot of fun."

Iris and George have been married for thirty-eight years and live in northern Colorado. George described their marriage like this: "We arrived at this season of marriage by fighting it out through the fall and winter seasons. Our early marriage was a bit of spring and that was fun, but this summer season is so much more joyful for us. We had to recommit continuously through our winters and falls. We made a decision early on that we would do whatever it took to work things out and move forward in our marriage, even though there were times when we didn't feel like it. Our strong sexual relationship helped keep us connected when our other communication was lacking. And I have to say that trusting in

God, reading Christian books on marriage, and attending marriage seminars have helped us more than anything."

Summer is an enjoyable season of marriage. The flowers are in full bloom. Sun-ripened fruits and vegetables are there to be enjoyed. Couples who want to remain in the summer season will take constructive actions, which grow out of positive attitudes and emotions. In summary, a summer marriage looks like this:

SUMMER	
EMOTIONS:	Happiness, satisfaction, accomplishment, connection
ATTITUDES:	Trust, commitment to growth, relaxed
ACTIONS:	Communicating constructively, accepting differences, attending seminars, reading books, growing spiritually
CLIMATE OF RELATIONSHIP:	Comfortable, attached, supportive, understanding. In the summer season of marriage, the dreams of spring have come true. Couples enjoy a great deal of satisfaction from their accomplishments. They are resolving conflicts in a positive manner. Having accepted their differences, they are seeking to turn them into assets for their relationship. Husbands and wives have a growing sense of togetherness.

THE DOWNSIDE OF SUMMER

Before we leave our discussion of summer, I must warn you about the yellow jackets. Last summer, as I was pulling some weeds down by the creek, I apparently ventured too close to the door of an underground nest. Before I knew it, I was under attack by a battalion of yellow jackets. I ran for my life and they pursued. Before I reached the safety of the house, I'd been stung fourteen times, which caused me intense pain for several hours.

In a summer marriage, the yellow jackets are analogous to those unresolved conflicts that nest beneath the surface of our day-to-day lives. We might be in the summer season of marriage, enjoying life together, watching the flowers bloom, doing a bit of weeding around the edges of our relationship; but there's another, unseen, level in our relationship, an underground nest where we have pushed our unresolved issues. When one spouse or the other ventures too close to the door of the nest, the yellow jackets come flying out and we find ourselves arguing in the middle of summer. When we look at Strategy 4, we will find practical ideas on how to get rid of the yellow jackets. For the moment, however, I simply want you to be aware that they exist and must be dealt with if you intend to continue living in the summer season of marriage.

47

Summer is my favorite time of the year and my favorite season of marriage. Karolyn and I spend most of our time in the summer season, but it has not always been that way. In the early years of our marriage, we spent a significant amount of time in the coldness of winter, punctuated with a few short springs and many extended fall seasons. It took us a long time to get to summer. Perhaps that's why when we finally got there, we wanted to make our marriage an eternal summer. I can't say that we've reached that objective, but we do spend more time in summer than in any of the other seasons.

In any marriage, summer can easily move into fall, almost before the couple recognize it. Fall is not as traumatic as winter, but it is not nearly as pleasant as summer. In the next chapter, we will describe the fall season of a marriage. We'll look at the emotions, the attitudes, and the actions that lead a couple to conclude that "the leaves are falling off our marriage and the flowers have definitely wilted."

FALL

In North Carolina and many other parts of the world, fall is the most colorful season of the year. The hills are painted with huge swatches of yellow, red, orange, and burgundy. Botanists can explain the natural causes of this sudden change of color, but most people simply enjoy it as nature's work of art. Thousands of people will drive to the mountains of western North Carolina during the fall season simply "to see the leaves."

What we do not talk about, but know without a doubt, is that this display of color is temporary. Soon the chilling winds will rip the vibrant canvas apart and the leaves will fall to the ground, leaving the trees bare. One interesting phenomenon is that the leaves do not all fall on the same day; but over a period of four to six weeks, the beauty fades and the forest is left unclothed. No one drives to the mountains to see a naked tree.

The falling of the leaves is an apt analogy of what happens in the fall season of marriage. In early fall, the marriage looks fine externally. Outsiders may even comment on how happy the couple seem to be. But inside the marriage, things are changing. And when the chilling winds arrive, the deterioration of the marriage will be obvious to all. Fall becomes the prelude to winter. As with the other seasons of marriage, fall has its own set of emotions, attitudes, and actions.

THE EMOTIONS OF FALL

The emotions of fall include feelings of sadness, apprehension, and rejection, sometimes accompanied by a feeling of being emotionally depleted. Couples in the fall season are aware that things aren't right, though they may or may not be expressing these feelings to each other. But they are troubled by the state of their relationship.

Marge is fifty-three and has been married for thirty-two years. Listen to the emotional words she uses as she describes her marriage as being in the fall season: "I feel a lot of insecurity about my marriage. My husband doesn't seem to be aware of what is going on, but I am very unhappy. We had put the children, Rick's job, and others above each other. Consequently, now that the children are gone, it seems like we are slipping apart. It's very scary, and I'm not sure what to do about it. Sometimes I feel overwhelmed."

I met Kimberly in Little Rock, Arkansas. She had been married for twenty years but was obviously troubled about her marriage. "I think we are in the late stages of fall and getting close to winter," she said.

"What does it feel like to be in the fall season of marriage?" I asked.

"Confusing, kind of scary, frustrating, burned out, and very stressful," she replied. She went on to describe the marriage and tell me what she thought had contributed to her feelings of distress. Her husband, who was listening to our conversation, did not offer any comments. When I looked at him and asked, "What does it feel like to you?" he had a one-word answer: "Bad."

Marvin is fifty-three and has been married for thirty-one years. He described his emotions in the following way: "I feel dejected, disheartened, and unappreciated. It's not a good place to be. I am not content with my marriage. Something has got to change or we're not going to make it." Marvin is in the late stages of fall. Winter will surely come if there are not significant changes. The encouraging note was that he said, "I believe that my wife and I will both benefit from the seminar, and we have purchased a number of books that we intend to read. I hope they will help us refocus our relationship."

Sometimes fall comes early in a marriage. Jackie and Charles had been married for eighteen years, but they had an early onset of fall in their relationship, "even though we got married in June," Jackie said. "Charles began rejecting me the day we got married. He has had at least one affair that he has admitted. Last year, he went into a deep depression. Through all the talking and counseling, he was diagnosed with a depressive disorder and codependency. He has very negative feelings toward his mother, who is now deceased, and he took all those feelings out on me. It has been like an emotional roller coaster for eighteen years. There have been some good moments, but mostly we have lived in fall. Only recently have I seen any hope. At least Charles was willing to go with me to a marriage seminar. And he has been willing to discuss a marriage book with me, so maybe there is hope."

When I asked Charles, "How do you feel about your marriage?" he said, "Afraid, but hoping for improvement with God's help."

I could cite numerous other examples of couples in the fall season of marriage, but perhaps these few are enough to give you a flavor of the emotions of fall: fear, sadness, rejection, and loneliness. These emotions may also be accompanied by feelings of dejection, a lack of appreciation, and resentment toward the spouse. Stephanie, who has been married for nineteen years and has a debilitating disease, summarized the emotions of fall: "I feel lonely, scared, uncertain, and frightened. I'm not sure how to handle all the emotions that come with overwhelming changes, a dire prognosis, and constant physical pain. We have not learned to handle our emotions together, so I am left alone, emotionally tired."

THE ATTITUDES OF FALL

The primary attitude of the fall season of marriage is one of great concern about the state of the marriage and uncertainty about where things are going. Most people do not want to be living in the fall season of marriage; therefore, they are concerned. They recognize that many changes are taking place, and they feel uncomfortable with what might be happening to their relationship.

Ginger, who is thirty-one and has been married almost seven years, said, "I'm very uncertain about our relationship. I'm hoping that we have now put God at the center of our marriage, but I have never been so unsure about myself, my spouse, and our marriage. God is why we are still together and trying. I am not content with this season. We are currently in Christian counseling. Looking back, I realize we have never really spoken one another's love language. We read the book and learned about them, but we didn't effectively speak them. Then my husband had a five-month affair with a coworker. He vehemently denied all my suspicions until he finally confessed. By the grace of God, we are still together and allowing God to work, reveal, and heal. In God's strength, we hope to finally become what he intended."

Harriett has been married for twenty years. She lives in a small town outside Atlanta, Georgia. She said, "Many changes are taking place in our lives. Our oldest daughter is graduating from high school and will soon be leaving. Many years of our marriage have been centered around our children. We have realized that, somewhere along the way, all our focus has been on our children and not really on each other. What are we going to do? My husband, in filling out his survey, wrote, 'We are in the summer season of our marriage.' Do we live in the same world? Sometimes I wonder. I am very concerned about our marriage."

Joan and Will have been married only eight months but describe their marriage as being in the fall season. Joan said, "It is fearful. I would like for it to change. There is a lot of doubt as to where I fit into Will's life and whether or not he even loves me. His family was allowed to interfere during the first few months of our marriage, and trust was broken or never created. We are now trying to follow Scripture's advice about 'leaving parents and cleaving to each other' in order to restore our relationship. I pray daily for deliverance from my insecurities."

Will described the marriage like this: "I am greatly hopeful, but times are very trying. I know we will come out on top and lead a happy life, but currently we argue almost every day. We are learning how to love and care for each other. The Lord is helping us in this process. I am excited about what I have heard at the marriage seminar and hope we can put it into practice. We had a very rocky start, but we are learning more how to show our love for each other. I am hoping we can move from fall back into spring and begin to build our marriage on a solid foundation." If Will and Joan can turn these hopes into reality, they can discover spring again.

Patrick and Tricia have been married for nineteen years. Because he is in the military, they have lived in many different places.

53

He says, "Our marriage has suffered late fall and early winter. This last year we have worked hard to recover, and we are digging our way out to head back to spring. My being sent to Iraq for a year showed both of us what we could lose. We are making progress by communicating, praying, and reading Christian books. I'm trying to become the spiritual leader of our family and show my wife how much I love her."

His wife, Tricia, described the marriage like this: "We are rebuilding our marriage after being apart because my husband was in Iraq for a year. It feels a little scary, but I know that we will grow closer, because throughout this year apart, we each drew closer to Christ. Only God could have healed a marriage like ours. Prior to Patrick's leaving to go to Iraq, we were eaten up with apathy and pride. It took his being away for me to appreciate him and to realize what a treasure the Lord has given me in him. Every day is one step closer to God's design for us as a married couple."

Obviously, some of these couples have greater hope than others. All of them have a degree of uncertainty; all are greatly concerned about their marriage. Whether they move from fall to winter or from fall to spring will depend largely upon the actions they choose to take.

THE ACTIONS OF FALL

In this section, I want to address both the actions that lead couples into the fall season of marriage and the actions that lead them out. Without a doubt, the number one contributor to the fall season of marriage—overwhelmingly—is the action of *neglect,* or taking no action at all. The underlying assumption seems to be that the marriage will take care of itself. Husbands and wives have their own separate interests, and they forget to do the kinds of things that foster a positive marital relationship.

Consequently, they grow slowly apart. They may be jolted into the reality that their marriage is in the fall season by some crisis, such as an extramarital affair, but the reality is that they were in the fall season for weeks—and perhaps months—before the crisis came. The leaves had changed color and were slowly falling from the branches, but they failed to recognize it because they were not in tune with each other. How they respond to the crisis will either push them into winter or lead them back toward spring.

Over and over again, in the research that I did in preparation for this book, couples who described their marriages as being in the fall season echoed that neglecting each other was the central ingredient in creating the fall season.

Kimberly from Little Rock, whom we met earlier in this chapter, described her feelings after twenty years of marriage as "confusing, kind of scary, frustrating, burned out, and very stressful." When I asked, "What do you think brought you to this season of marriage?" she replied, "Lack of communication, not spending time together, having nothing in common, leading separate lives. This led to substance-abuse issues, unfaithfulness, lies, and lack of trust." It is interesting to note the progression of distance that developed between Kimberly and her husband, but it began with large-scale neglect.

Marvin is the husband we met earlier who felt "dejected, disheartened, and unappreciated." In describing how he arrived in the fall season of marriage, he said, "I think that the main problem has been lack of communication. We have been so busy having and raising our three children and making a living that we have not made time with each other a priority. Therefore, we grew apart."

Mildred, who lives in Spokane, Washington, and has been married for thirty-three years, described her marriage as "not good. I know the marriage will remain and survive, but I want it to be tender and growing. The kids grew up, left home, and started their own families. When they left, my husband and I no longer had that common focus; we tended to do our own thing and grew apart. We simply neglected our relationship."

Carol from Baton Rouge, Louisiana, echoed those sentiments: "I have been married to my second husband for twelve years, and we have neglected to nurture our marriage. We have turned our attention totally to our children, ignoring each other's needs. In so doing, we have done ourselves and our children a disservice. The state of our marriage is a great disappointment. But I believe the foundation is still there. My husband is open, and we are trying to rebuild our relationship."

Without question, neglect is what leads couples into the fall season of marriage. When a husband and wife allow the relationship to drift, they will always drift apart. When they drift apart, life becomes uncertain and scary. When couples realize they are in the fall season of marriage, they have a choice: They can take positive actions that lead back to spring or summer, or they can make destructive choices that lead to winter and possibly the death of the marriage.

One of the actions that perpetuate fall or lead to winter is a failure to seek resolution of issues. Marti, from Fort Wayne, Indiana, illustrated this dilemma. "We've been married for four years and I am very unhappy with our marriage. I just don't like Jon very much. I feel like I'm out of control and that is not familiar territory for me. He wants sex all the time, regardless of whether the kids are still awake or I'm right in the middle of cooking dinner. I need a few things to lead up to it . . . you know, kind words, a nice dinner, a quiet house. He doesn't care what else gets done around the house as long as we have sex. It was not this way from the beginning. I admit my response has been negative. I do not consciously withhold sex, but I realize that my resentment controls my actions. Sometimes we have gone months without sex. I'm not proud of that. I try to make conscious efforts to touch him, but he is never satisfied. I try to fill his love tank, but he never fills mine. I've been bitter, stubborn, and resentful. I know that something has got to change."

Marti is exactly right. *Something has got to change.* Unresolved issues will keep couples in the fall season of marriage—or, more likely, will lead them to winter.

Sexual infidelity is another factor that has the potential to move a fall marriage to the winter season. As Emily, from Norfolk, Virginia, said, "My heart is broken. After thirty-seven years of marriage, I never dreamed we would ever be in this situation. This is my husband's second affair that I am aware of. This time it is more serious than before. He's a partner in a successful business, very active in the community, and a respected elected official in our county. But I find it hard to respect him. He is an only child and became very selfish. We have three married daughters and six grandchildren, with one on the way. He is willing to lose it all for a very aggressive woman.

"We have tried counseling together. After the first session, he would not go back because he did not like the counselor. The second counselor told us he was wasting our money because my husband showed no remorse, guilt, or shame for what he was doing. He is now in counseling alone, I think. I pray for him and her many times a day. They both say they are Christians, but words are cheap. I have had about all I can take, but I am still praying and hoping that he will be willing to work on our marriage."

Emily's situation illustrates the reality that it takes both spouses to move a marriage from fall to spring, but it takes only one to move from fall to winter. The way we think and the actions we take make all the difference. The fall season of marriage is characterized by a sense of detaching. The leaves of our marriage are beginning to fall, and we are not certain what the future holds. It can be a very troubling time. Here is the summary of a fall marriage:

FALL	
EMOTIONS:	Fear, sadness, dejection, apprehension, discouragement, resentment, feelings of being unappreciated
ATTITUDES:	Concern, uncertainty, blaming
ACTIONS:	Neglect, failure to face issues
CLIMATE OF RELATIONSHIP:	Drifting apart, disengaging. In the fall season, couples sense that something is happening, but they're not sure what. There is a sense of detachment. One or both spouses begin to feel neglected. Couples realize there are some issues they are not facing squarely. It seems that they are disengaging emotionally, and each tends to blame the other. If they have lived in the fall season for a while, their friends and family may be recognizing the changes.

MAKING THE MOST OF FALL

Couples are often in the early stages of fall before they realize it. They have been busy with the activities of summer, enjoying life but sometimes ignoring each other. As the color of the leaves begins to change, externally the marriages still look good. Couples are living in the afterglow of summer, but internally each partner is slowly disengaging.

In the latter stage of fall the leaves are gone, and the emptiness of the relationship becomes apparent. It is this emotional emptiness that causes concern, uncertainty, and fearfulness. The dawning awareness of detachment often motivates one spouse or both to reach out for help. They may agree to attend a marriage seminar, seek the help of a counselor, or read and discuss a book about marriage. One young wife said, "I never thought I'd come for counseling, but I am so concerned about what is happening in our marriage. I know we need help, and I don't want to wait until it's too late." The uncertainties of fall can prove redemptive if the couple turn in the right direction.

Fall can lead directly into spring or a return to summer. On the other hand, if couples simply allow "nature to take its course," they will inevitably wake up in winter. In the second part of this book, we will look at specific strategies for making the most of the fall season of marriage.

Perhaps as you have read these introductory chapters, you have easily identified the season of your marriage. Or maybe you've had difficulty distinguishing between spring and summer or fall and winter. It is true that the late stages of fall and the early stages of winter are very similar. The same is true of the late stages of spring and the early stages of summer. But before we move on to discuss strategies for enhancing the seasons of your marriage, it is important for you to identify the season you're in. In the next chapter, you will find a seasonal profile that will help you make this determination.

The Marital Seasons Profile is not designed as a scientific instrument to force you into a seasonal category; rather, it is a communication tool to help you and your spouse take an honest look at your marriage. Whatever your conclusions about the season of your marriage, I think you will find the second part of the book extremely helpful in discovering or rediscovering the excitement of spring and the joys of summer. I hope you will also understand that the seasons of fall and winter are not altogether purposeless. They often serve as a wake-up call to stimulate marital growth. *No marriage is hopeless!* With the help of God, all things are possible.

MARITAL SEASONS
PROFILE

Marriage relationships are constantly changing. As we've seen, they go through identifiable seasons that may occur numerous times throughout the life of a marriage. That is, every couple will experience a succession of winters, summers, springs, and falls. The value of identifying the present season of your marriage is that it will help you become conscious of the present quality of your marriage and aware of the attitudes, emotions, and actions that characterize your relationship.

Some of the seasons of marriage are more enjoyable and productive than others. Knowing the season of your marriage will allow you to take positive steps to maintain the joys of spring and summer and correct the negative behaviors that lead to fall and winter. If both you and your spouse are willing to take the profile, it can be a means for the two of you to honestly discuss the quality of your marriage and to take positive steps in stimulating marital growth. It is recommended that you take the profile individually without discussion until you have tabulated your results. The following pages include a profile score sheet for each spouse.

MARITAL SEASONS INDICATOR

What season is your marriage in? Four words or phrases appear in each of the following sixteen rows. Choose one word or phrase per row that best represents your thoughts and feelings about your marriage during the past few weeks. Once you have checked one word or phrase per row, tally each of the four columns by counting each check mark in that column as one point. You will have a score ranging from 0 to 16 for each of the four columns. Instructions for interpreting your scores can be found on the next page.

1.	O Discouraging	O Exciting	O Satisfying	O Uncertain
2.	O Hopeless	O Happy	O Peaceful	O Confusing
3.	O Empty	O Hopeful	O Committed	O Stressful
4.	O Harsh	O Nurturing	O Secure	O Frustrating
5.	O Resentful	O Open	O Trusting	O Tired
6.	O Destructive	O Fresh	O Relaxed	O Distant
7.	O Rejection	O Anticipation	O Appreciation	O Apprehension
8.	O Tension	O Sharing	O Honest	O Drifting
9.	O Give up	O Making Plans	O Teamwork	O Apathetic
10.	O Critical	O Caring	O Connected	O Concerned
11.	O Angry	O Joyful	O Understanding	O Burned out
12.	O Disappointed	O Optimistic	O Comfortable	O Neglectful
13.	O Untrusting	O Tender	O Supportive	O Afraid
14.	O Withdrawn	O Growing	O Attached	O Detached
15.	O Cold	O Alive	O Content	O Prideful
16.	O Unforgiving	O Willing to change	O Overlook flaws	O Growing apart
	Column 1 Total	Column 2 Total	Column 3 Total	Column 4 Total

INTERPRETING YOUR SCORES

As you may have guessed, column 1 lists words and phrases that are typically used to describe the winter season of marriage. Column 2 represents spring. Column 3 represents summer. Column 4 represents fall. The column with the most points reflects the current season of your marriage. A close or equal score between two seasons suggests your marriage has elements of both seasons or may be in transition. The highest possible score for any season is 16. If you scored a 16, it indicates that your marriage is deep in that season.

Do you agree with your scores? Are you surprised? On the next page, you'll find a second Marital Seasons Indicator for your spouse to complete. Afterward, the two of you will be able to compare your answers and discuss what you each have contributed, either positive or negative, to bring you into this season. If you are in an enjoyable season, congratulations and keep up the good work! The second part of this book will teach you some strategies to keep your marriage growing and thriving. If you are not in an enjoyable season, don't give up. The strategies explained in Part II will give you some practical steps you can take to improve your marriage. Regardless of the season of your marriage, there's hope and there's room for improvement. Commit yourself to work for the best possible marriage you can have.

MARITAL SEASONS INDICATOR FOR YOUR SPOUSE

What season is your marriage in? Four words or phrases appear in each of the following sixteen rows. Choose one word or phrase per row that best represents your thoughts and feelings about your marriage during the past few weeks. Once you have checked one word or phrase per row, tally each of the four columns by counting each check mark in that column as one point. You will have a score ranging from 0 to 16 for each of the four columns. Instructions for interpreting your scores can be found on the next page.

	Column 1	Column 2	Column 3	Column 4
1.	○ Discouraging	○ Exciting	○ Satisfying	○ Uncertain
2.	○ Hopeless	○ Happy	○ Peaceful	○ Confusing
3.	○ Empty	○ Hopeful	○ Committed	○ Stressful
4.	○ Harsh	○ Nurturing	○ Secure	○ Frustrating
5.	○ Resentful	○ Open	○ Trusting	○ Tired
6.	○ Destructive	○ Fresh	○ Relaxed	○ Distant
7.	○ Rejection	○ Anticipation	○ Appreciation	○ Apprehension
8.	○ Tension	○ Sharing	○ Honest	○ Drifting
9.	○ Give up	○ Making Plans	○ Teamwork	○ Apathetic
10.	○ Critical	○ Caring	○ Connected	○ Concerned
11.	○ Angry	○ Joyful	○ Understanding	○ Burned out
12.	○ Disappointed	○ Optimistic	○ Comfortable	○ Neglectful
13.	○ Untrusting	○ Tender	○ Supportive	○ Afraid
14.	○ Withdrawn	○ Growing	○ Attached	○ Detached
15.	○ Cold	○ Alive	○ Content	○ Prideful
16.	○ Unforgiving	○ Willing to change	○ Overlook flaws	○ Growing apart
	—	—	—	—
	Column 1 Total	Column 2 Total	Column 3 Total	Column 4 Total
	_____	_____	_____	_____

INTERPRETING YOUR SCORES

As you may have guessed, column 1 lists words and phrases that are typically used to describe the winter season of marriage. Column 2 represents spring. Column 3 represents summer. Column 4 represents fall. The column with the most points reflects the current season of your marriage. A close or equal score between two seasons suggests your marriage has elements of both seasons or may be in transition. The highest possible score for any season is 16. If you scored a 16, it indicates that your marriage is deep in that season.

Do you agree with your scores? Are you surprised? Compare your answers with your spouse's answers and discuss what you each have contributed, either positive or negative, to bring you into this season. If you are in an enjoyable season, congratulations and keep up the good work! The second part of this book will teach you some strategies to keep your marriage growing and thriving. If you are not in an enjoyable season, don't give up. The strategies explained in Part II will give you some practical steps you can take to improve your marriage. Regardless of the season of your marriage, there's hope and there's room for improvement. Commit yourself to work for the best possible marriage you can have.

PART II

Seven Strategies to Enhance the Seasons of Your Marriage

*N*ow that we understand the characteristics of the four seasons of marriage, let's turn our attention to seven strategies that can move your marriage from the cold of winter to the warmth of summer; from the uncertainty of fall to the excitement of spring; or enhance the quality of your marriage, regardless of season. These biblically based strategies have grown out of my counseling experience over the past thirty years. I have seen numerous marriages turn in a positive direction by applying these ideas. They are not necessarily designed to be used in numerical order, although dealing with past failures (Strategy 1) often clears the debris in a relationship and paves the way for implementing the other strategies.

Each strategy holds the potential to enhance the season of your marriage. I suggest that you read all seven strategies and then go back and select the one that seems the most appropriate to implement first. If your spouse is willing to join you, then what you learn and apply from the next seven chapters could be the beginning of a whole new way of relating to each other. If, on the other hand, your spouse wants "nothing to do with that *Seasons* book," you may find Strategy 7 extremely valuable.

If you are in the spring or summer season of marriage, these strategies will give you practical ideas for keeping your marriage alive and growing. If you are in the fall or winter season of marriage, these strategies can get your relationship moving toward a warmer, more pleasant season. Marriages either grow or they regress; they never stand still. Your attitudes and actions will affect your emotions as well as your spouse's. These strategies will challenge you to develop positive attitudes and actions that will greatly enhance the emotional climate of your marriage.

STRATEGY 1

Deal with Past Failures

Every married couple needs to understand this strategy, but couples in the fall or winter seasons of marriage will need to spend more time here identifying and processing past failures. Most of us can identify with Brent, who said, "I know I have had failures in the past. Both of us have failed; but why can't we forget the past and focus on the present and the future?" I am deeply empathetic with Brent's desire, but it doesn't work that way. We have to deal with the past before we can put it behind us. Otherwise, it keeps popping back up. But once we have resolved our past failures, we can spend our energy focusing on the present and create better seasons in the future. The strategy outlined in this chapter is one I have used with hundreds of couples through the years to help them deal realistically with past failures. I am confident that it will also work for you.

Dealing with past failures involves three steps: identifying past failures, confession and repentance, and forgiveness. The first step may be the most difficult.

STEP 1: IDENTIFYING PAST FAILURES

The first step in dealing with past failures is to identify them. When I shared this idea with Brent, he said, "Oh, I don't have any problem with that. Helen rehearses my failures every time we get into an argument."

"Perhaps," I said, "but my guess is she doesn't list even thirty percent of your failures. No doubt her criticism irritates you. You're tired of hearing about your shortcomings, and you want her to forget about them. But the fact is you haven't done the hard work of identifying your own failures."

Brent wasn't very happy with my initial approach, so he said, "But what about her? Doesn't she have failures, too?"

"Absolutely. I don't even know your wife yet, but I'm certain she has had failures because she's human. But right now I'm talking to you, and you have expressed a desire that she would 'forget the past and live in the present with a view to making the future better.' I'm telling you how that can happen. And it begins with *you*."

My straightforward approach with Brent was based on a discovery I've made in my years as a marriage counselor. The reality is that most of us can identify our spouse's failures much more readily than we can identify our own. Jesus described the problem in Matthew 7:3-5. If we apply his teaching to marriage, it would sound like this: "Why do you look at the speck of sawdust in your spouse's eye and pay no attention to the plank in your own eye? . . . First take the plank out of your own eye, and then you will see clearly to remove the speck from your spouse's eye."

When I read those verses to Brent's wife, Helen, several weeks later, she said, "But that's not the way it is in our marriage. Brent doesn't have a *speck* in his eye, he has hundreds of *logs*. I know I'm not perfect, but he's the real problem in our marriage."

"Perhaps you are right," I said. "However, because you are a follower of Jesus, would you be willing to start where Jesus told us to start—namely, by dealing with your own failures?" When she didn't immediately respond, I added, "I'll commit myself to helping Brent deal with *his* failures if you will commit yourself to deal with your own."

"I'm willing to do that," Helen said, "but I just want you to know where the real problem is."

I let her statement pass without comment and said, "Okay, here is your assignment for this week: I want you to set aside two hours to get alone with God. Take your Bible, a notebook, and a pen or pencil, and I want you to pray a very biblical prayer. It is a prayer of David's, found in Psalm 139:23-24. As you know, David had lots of failures in his life. Here is his prayer: 'Search me, O God, and know my heart; test me and know my anxious thoughts. See if there is any offensive way in me, and lead me in the way everlasting.' Ask God to show you specific ways and times in which you have failed Brent over the past seventeen years. You may even start with your courtship and engagement period, then move through the wedding, the honeymoon, the first year of your marriage, and so on. Ask God to bring to your mind the times when you spoke harshly to him or withdrew in silence, the times when you did hurtful things or treated him unkindly. As you listen to God, I want you to make a list of everything he brings to your mind.

"I want to warn you, though, that Satan will also try to speak to your mind. His message will go something like this: 'Well, certainly you were not kind, but that's because of what Brent did to you. That's not your fault. That doesn't count.' Satan does not want you to be honest. He wants you to blame others for your own sinful behavior. Remember, Adam and Eve listened to

71

Satan's voice. Adam blamed Eve, and Eve blamed the serpent. If we are going to deal with past failures, we must identify them and be willing to accept the responsibility for our own wrongful behavior."

Helen indicated that she understood the assignment. "However," she said, "two hours is a long time. I don't think it will take that long."

"Don't short-circuit the process," I cautioned. "Set aside the two hours, and at least every fifteen minutes ask God to show you more of your failures."

"Okay," she said, "but I don't think it will take two hours." I sensed that Helen felt I was not dealing with the real problem, but she was willing to go along with my strategy.

The following week Helen returned with her list. "I found more things than I thought. But they are mainly little things, and I've asked God to forgive me."

"No, no, no," I said. "We're not ready for that."

"What do you mean?" she asked. "Aren't we supposed to confess our sins to God?"

"Yes, but first we've got to identify them."

"Well, that's what I did," she said.

"No, no, no. You took the first step. This week I have another assignment. I want you to talk with each of your children individually. Tell them that you are working on your marriage. Tell them that you are trying to identify your failures in the marriage and that you want them to tell you of the times they remember when you spoke harshly to Brent, when you treated him unkindly and unfairly. Tell them that you want them to be totally truthful because you know you cannot work on your marriage if you are not honest.

"Then, I want you to go to your parents individually and ask them the same question. I understand that you and Brent have Sunday lunch with them once a month. Is that correct?" Helen nodded. "So they have had a fair amount of exposure to the two of you together. Ask them what they remember about times when they have heard you do or say things that were harsh or unloving to Brent. Then I want you to go to Brent's parents individually and make the same request."

Helen was visibly irritated. "I don't know where all of this is leading, and I don't know why I need to do all this, especially since Brent's failures are the real problem in our marriage."

"I can understand why you might be frustrated with my approach," I said, "but let me remind you that I'm meeting with Brent every week and I'm giving him the same assignments I'm giving you. Marriage is a two-way street. Neither of you is perfect, and each of you must deal with your own failures. The first step is to identify those failures and take responsibility for them. To this point, neither you nor Brent has done this. However, it appears to me that now, for the first time in your lives, both of you are very serious about wanting to deal with the past failures in your marriage. And we are following a biblical pattern of beginning with our own failures."

Helen took a deep breath and said, "I know. You're right. We've got to deal with this. But bringing the kids in on this and my parents and his parents—how can that be helpful?"

"They are the people who know you best," I said. "And they are concerned about your marriage. In doing this, you are demonstrating to the children your sincerity and your honesty. And you are giving them a chance to voice what they have observed through the years about your behavior. Your parents and his parents will be glad to know that you are trying to deal with your part. And when Brent does his assignment, they will see that he is trying to deal with his part. God can use this process not only for your benefit but also for the benefit of your parents, your in-laws, and your children."

There may be exceptions to the idea of consulting children, parents, and in-laws. For example, preschool children may be too young; dysfunctional parents or in-laws may be obsessively prejudiced and find it difficult to be objective. However you can best accomplish it in your own relationship, the point is to broaden your perspective beyond your own self-protective viewpoint. Often, hearing something from a child, a parent, or another close family member can really open our eyes to how we are treating our mate.

Marriage doesn't operate in a vacuum. It affects everyone who is closely associated with a couple. I can assure you that you are likely to hear some things from your children and parents that you don't want to hear. Satan will tell you to defend yourself and say that what they are saying is not really the whole picture. He will want you to discount their testimony. Don't yield to that temptation. They are giving you good information. It is their perception of what they have observed about the way you have treated your spouse. Perhaps it was not your intention, but that's the way it came across to them. So accept what they say and put it on your list.

When I gave Helen this assignment, I said, "I'm going to give you two weeks to do this, because it will take some time."

"Okay, but it's also going to be really hard."

"You're right," I agreed. "It's never easy to ask those who know us best to give us honest feedback about our failures. It is very difficult but highly profitable."

Before the two weeks were up, Helen called and asked for a one-week extension. When she came in the next time, however, she had completed the assignment thoroughly. "I didn't know that my children and my parents and in-laws had observed so much about my behavior. I was shocked about some of the things they said—and a little upset. But I remembered your challenge not to be defensive, so I wasn't. I listened and I wrote and I've got a pretty long list. I feel bad that the children picked up on my harshness to Brent through the years. In my mind, he deserved it. But I know it was not good for them to hear me talk to their father like I did." I could tell that Helen was beginning to identify and take responsibility for her failures.

"So what am I going to do with this list?" she asked. "I've already asked God to forgive me."

"That's fine," I said, "but we're not quite ready for that. There's one more step. When we began this process, you told me that the real problem is Brent and not you. Remember? I have no reason to doubt what you said. So this week I want you to make a list of all the ways that Brent has hurt you through the years."

"There won't be enough paper," she said, laughing and crying at the same time.

I nodded and offered her some encouragement. "I know that you have been hurt through the years by Brent's actions. If that were not true, you would not be in my office for counseling. So I want to give you a chance to share these hurts with Brent—but here is the spirit in which I want you to share them."

I handed her a sheet of paper that had the following paragraph printed at the top:

> *Dear Brent,*
> *I want to thank you for joining me in getting counseling for our marriage. As you know, Dr. Chapman has been helping us identify and take responsibility for our own failures. I can*

assure you that I have a pretty long list by now of ways in which I have failed you. This week we have been asked to make a list of the hurts we have experienced through the years. I know that many of these you have heard before because I tend to bring them up every time we get into an argument. I am writing this list not because I hate you but because I love you. And I want us to be able to put the past behind us so that we can build a better future. The first thing that comes to mind is . . .

I asked Helen to read the paragraph and tell me if she agreed with it. When she responded positively, I said, "Now, I want you to write the first sentence sitting right here in the office. What is the first thing that comes to your mind?"

"Well, chronologically," she said, "it's when he forgot our first anniversary. But the most painful was when he had an emotional fling with a girl at the office."

"And which do you want to put first?" I asked.

"I'll go chronologically."

"Okay, here's the way I want you to begin. You write as I talk. Number one: 'I felt . . .' How would you describe your feelings when he forgot your first anniversary?"

Helen sat for a moment before beginning to write. When she finished, I read this sentence: "I felt disappointed and deeply hurt on our first anniversary when the day came and went and you never mentioned it. I kept thinking you would surprise me with something, but you never did. As you remember, we ended up arguing half the night. I know I said some horrible things that night, but they grew out of my deep hurt. I couldn't believe you had forgotten the day we got married."

"Now," I said, "I want you to begin each sentence with the

words *I felt* and describe your feelings when Brent did something or said something or failed to do something or say something that hurt you. Don't preach to him. Just tell him how you felt about the event. You may list everything you remember. They don't have to be in chronological order, but I want your list to be as comprehensive as possible."

"This could take a long time," Helen said, laughing.

"That's fine," I responded. "How many weeks do you want?"

"I think two will be sufficient."

"All right, then I'll see you in two weeks."

Two weeks later, I read through Helen's list of thirty-five painful experiences. I helped her rewrite two of them because she had started the sentence with *You made me feel,* rather than *I felt.* I reminded Helen that our purpose was not to condemn Brent but rather to inform him of her feelings. She had the list saved on her computer, so the revisions were not a major task. The next day, she dropped off her corrected list at my office.

The following week, I gave Helen's list to Brent and Brent's list to Helen. "Read the list as *information from the heart of your spouse,*" I challenged both of them. "I want you to sense what your spouse was *feeling* when these events occurred. I assume that your intention was not to hurt each other, but in reality both of you have experienced a great deal of pain. In dealing with the past, I want both of you to be aware of how your actions have hurt the other person. And I want you to take responsibility for that pain. Again, I don't mean that you intended to hurt your mate, but the reality is that he or she was deeply affected by your behavior.

"As you read through the list your spouse has given you, examine the list you made of your own failures to see if all your spouse's hurts are included on your list. If not, I want you to add them."

The process of identifying past failures takes time and effort. It may also be painful. However, we cannot deal with past failures until we know what they are. Bringing family members into the process helps us see what others have observed about our behavior. We seldom see ourselves as others see us. Writing out our own pain from past experiences helps us identify why we are so hurt and angry. Sharing it with our spouse in written form makes it easier for him or her to sense our pain and not get defensive.

STEP 2: CONFESSION AND REPENTANCE

Once Brent and Helen had exchanged lists of hurts and had amended their own list of failures, they were ready for the second step in the strategy of dealing with past failures: confession and repentance, first to God and then to each other. I encouraged each of them to set aside another two hours to get alone with God, their Bible, and their lists. "Begin by reading Psalm 51," I suggested. "This is David's confession after he was confronted by Nathan the prophet and realized how deeply he had failed God and others. Let his prayer be a model for your own prayer. I want you to go through your list and confess each thing to God."

The word *confession* means "to agree with." Therefore, when you confess your failures and admit that you have hurt your spouse, you are agreeing with God that you were wrong. You are agreeing that your behavior has caused pain to your spouse and has grieved God's heart. *Repentance* means "to turn around and walk in the opposite direction." By repenting of your failures and the hurt you've caused your spouse, you are expressing to God your desire to behave differently in the future. You are asking for the power of the Holy Spirit to enable you to love your spouse as God intends.

Scripture says, "If we confess our sins [to God], he is faithful and just and will forgive us our sins and purify us from all unrighteousness" (1 John 1:9). When we confess our sins and repent, God is fully willing to forgive us. And he is able to forgive us because Christ has paid the penalty for our sin. Therefore, God can maintain his justice, yet still forgive the sinner, because Christ already paid the penalty (see Romans 5:8-11).

Having confessed and repented to God, Brent and Helen then were to do the same with each other. "This next week," I said, "spend two hours with each other going through the list of your own failures. Acknowledge to each other, line by line, that you were wrong and that you're sorry you hurt each other so deeply. And then ask for forgiveness.

"Don't rush through the list," I cautioned them. "Take time with each item. Let your spouse hear you verbalize that you were wrong and that you feel bad that you hurt him or her so deeply."

The second instruction I gave Helen and Brent was this: "Don't judge the other person's sincerity. We have different personalities. Some people, for example, cry more readily than others. Don't expect your spouse to exhibit the same body language that you do. He or she may be more stoic but just as sincere. Choose to receive your mate's words as a sincere, heartfelt confession and apology. Express your intention that, with the help of God, you hope to make things better in the future."

STEP 3: FORGIVENESS

Now Brent and Helen were ready for true forgiveness. In the Scriptures, forgiveness is always the Christian response to confession and repentance. Jesus said, "If your brother sins, rebuke

79

him, and if he repents, forgive him" (Luke 17:3). There is no place in the Christian life for an unforgiving spirit. In fact, Jesus taught that an unforgiving spirit is rebellion against God and must be confessed as sinful.[1]

I said to Brent and Helen, "Remember, forgiveness is not a feeling. It is a decision to lift the penalty for past failures and declare the spouse pardoned. Forgiveness does not mean that you will never think of the event again, nor does it mean that you will never feel the pain that accompanies the memory. Forgiveness does mean that you will no longer hold that failure or hurt against your spouse. As 1 Corinthians 13:5 says, love 'keeps no record of wrongs.'"

Forgiveness means that we don't bring up past failures. It means we recognize that Christ has already paid the penalty for our sins. When we have confessed and repented to God and to each other—and God has forgiven us—we choose to forgive each other.

The strategy of dealing with past failures applies to all four seasons of marriage, because all of us have failures that need to be confessed and forgiven. Couples in the season of winter or fall may have huge storehouses of past failures that have never been processed. Couples in the season of spring or summer will need to deal with failures that occur as a part of the normal flow of life and not allow these to be stored and become a barrier to intimacy.

The thought of dealing with past failures may strike terror in some individuals. I remember the husband who said, "She hasn't mentioned it in six months; I'm hoping she's forgotten it. I certainly don't want to bring it up again myself." The fact that he was afraid to bring up the subject indicated it had never been fully confessed and forgiven. Whether his wife ever mentions it again or not, it is one of those underground yellow jackets that is likely to come out and sting him.

I know that dealing with past failures will be really hard for some people, but the benefits of identification, confession, repentance, and forgiveness are so enormous that it will be worth the effort. If you're stuck here, consider these three benefits:

① You will no longer fear the past because you have confessed your failures and have been forgiven.

② Your marriage relationship will be deepened when you and your spouse experience genuine confession, repentance, and forgiveness. Forgiveness makes possible the restoration of your marriage relationship.

③ In forgiving others, you become more like Christ. In other words, dealing with past failures is a huge step toward spiritual maturity.

Brent and Helen followed Strategy 1, a major step in moving from winter to spring. In fact, for the two of them, spring returned almost immediately, and they began making plans for a new future. I warned them, of course, that they were still not perfect and that one of them might revert to old patterns and bring up a past failure in the heat of anger. "But when that happens," I said, "recognize it as sinful behavior, confess it to God and to your spouse as quickly as possible, and ask forgiveness."

I am often asked, "What if my spouse is not willing to follow a strategy such as dealing with the past?" I will answer that question more fully in Strategy 7, but let me say briefly here that you can influence your spouse by your own behavior. When you choose

81

to follow a biblical strategy, you will have a positive influence on your spouse. You cannot control your spouse's behavior, but you can—and do—greatly influence him or her by your own behavior. Following biblical strategies is the most powerful way to influence a nonparticipating spouse.

STRATEGY 2

Choose a Winning Attitude

Most athletes would agree that winning is ninety percent attitude and ten percent hard work. If that is true in the world of sports, it is certainly also true in the world of relationships. Spring and summer marriages are created and sustained by positive attitudes. Fall and winter marriages are characterized by negative attitudes. What we *think* largely influences what we *do*. In turn, our actions greatly influence our emotions. This connection between attitude and actions opens a door of hope for all couples. If we can change our thinking, we can change the season of our marriage.

The most common mistake couples make is allowing negative emotions to dictate their behavior. By failing to recognize the power of a positive attitude, they fail to achieve their marriage's highest potential.

We have long recognized the power of a positive attitude in the business arena. Consider the attitudes of two different salespeople. One thinks, *These people need a vacuum cleaner. I have the best one on the market and if I can show it to them, I know they will want it. And I can help them find a way to get it.* The other one thinks, *These people would not be interested in buying a vacuum cleaner. They have too many other things on their minds. Besides that, they couldn't afford one if they wanted it.* Which salesperson is more likely to succeed? In this chapter I want to help you develop your potential for positive thinking, which will lead you to greater marital success.

I must confess that I learned this strategy the hard way. Earlier in my marriage, I spent a great deal of time in the winter season because of my negative attitudes. And when I was in the midst of winter, I found it hard to admit that my attitude was part of the problem. It was much easier to blame Karolyn's behavior for our poor marriage. Today, I readily admit that my negative thinking was the culprit. If you are living in the fall or winter season of marriage, my guess is that you, too, have the tendency to blame your spouse and are failing to recognize your own negative attitudes. If you want to break free from the coldness and bitterness of winter, I challenge you to devour the truth in this chapter. Changing your attitude can be a catalyst that sets in motion a seasonal change for your marriage.

Circumstances are neutral—or at least they're common. Therefore, it is not what happens to us but how we *interpret* what happens to us (our attitude) that makes the difference between success and failure. Let me show you the difference in the lives of two couples: Betsy and Kirk, and Charles and Kelly.

Betsy and Kirk had been married twelve years when they experienced the death of their nine-year-old son. He was killed instantly by an automobile as he rode his bicycle from the driveway into the street. In my first conversation with Betsy, which occurred less than six hours after the accident, I discovered the seeds of blame. She said, "I had just told Kirk last week that he needs to spend more time with Andrew, talking with him about safety rules for riding his bicycle. If Kirk had talked with him, maybe this would not have happened."

Later, in talking with Kirk, I sensed a similar attitude. "I have never liked this place," he said. "I told Betsy two years ago that I wanted us to get a little farm. I don't like raising kids in the city. It's too dangerous. I wish I had listened to my heart." Two months later, in another conversation, I found Kirk rehearsing the same message again. "I just wish we would have moved to the farm two years ago. Betsy resisted the idea. She said it was so much more convenient in the city, but there is more to life than convenience."

The following week I met with Betsy and found that she, too, had been playing the same message in her mind for two months. "If only Kirk had talked to Andrew about safety rules, maybe Andrew would still be with us." Betsy was blaming Kirk, and Kirk was blaming Betsy. They would not have said it directly to one another, but their attitudes revealed the truth.

I wish I could say that through counseling Kirk and Betsy changed their attitudes and found comfort and hope. The reality is that in less than a year they were separated and shortly thereafter divorced, creating additional pain for their other two sons, ages five and seven. Negative attitudes led to negative behavior, which ended in bitterness and divorce.

Charles and Kelly experienced a very similar tragedy, but with very different results. Andrea, their seven-year-old daughter, drowned in the backyard pool while both parents were in the house. Charles and Kelly were planning to join Andrea for a swim, but she jumped in before they arrived. "She was a good swimmer," Kelly said, "and she had never gone into the pool without our being there. That was one of our rules. I don't know what happened."

I had several sessions with Kelly and Charles over the next six months. Never once did I hear them blame each other, and never once did they blame Andrea. "She was just being a child," Kelly said, with tears coursing down her cheeks. "No need to blame her for breaking our buddy rule. It won't bring her back." Deeply pained, Charles and Kelly talked their way through their grief, gave each other the freedom to cry, held each other tenderly, and survived the ordeal with an even stronger marriage.

"We had a good marriage," Charles said. "But the loss of Andrea has brought us even closer together. We know we can't bring her back, but we can go to be with her. We want to be good parents to our son and trust God with the future."

In the years since Andrea's death, Charles and Kelly have gone on to live fruitful, productive lives. God gave them two additional children, whom they are rearing in a very nurturing home.

The difference between the two couples was basically a difference in attitude. Both were deeply hurt; both suffered tragic loss. One couple chose an attitude of blame, whereas the other couple chose an attitude of acceptance and support. Attitude made all the difference. "God gave us Andrea, and we had her for seven wonderful years," Charles said. "She brought us great joy, and now she is in the presence of God. She loved Jesus. We loved her, and we know we will see her again someday. We know that she would not want us to sit around grieving her death for the next twenty years. As long as God gives us life, we want to be faithful in loving and caring for our other children and serving God." As Charles tried to summarize their attitude, Kelly was nodding her head affirmingly. Together they were demonstrating the power of a positive attitude in the midst of tragedy.

A Christian worldview—that is, a biblical perspective on life— makes it much easier for couples to have a positive mental attitude. Perhaps you are asking, "What is this 'Christian worldview' that fosters such a positive attitude?" Let me mention some of the characteristics.

First is the recognition that every human being is made in the image of God and is therefore extremely valuable. Second, each

---

CHARACTERISTICS OF A CHRISTIAN WORLDVIEW

Every human being is made in the image of God and is therefore extremely valuable.

Each person is uniquely gifted by God (including the mentally and physically challenged).

Each person has a unique role to play in life.

Marriage is God's idea. Husbands and wives are intended to complement each other.

The object of marriage is to glorify God by serving one's spouse and helping the spouse reach his or her God-given potential.

---

person is uniquely gifted by God (including the mentally and physically challenged). Third, each person has a unique role to play in life. Fourth, marriage is God's idea. Thus, a man and a woman are uniquely created to work together as a team. Each has strengths and weaknesses. Each is called upon to comple-ment the other. If they learn how to do this, they will accom-plish more than they would ever have accomplished as individuals. Fifth, the goal of marriage is that husbands and wives voluntarily serve each other, helping each other reach their potential for God and promoting good in the world. When I meditate on these five truths, I am drawn to a positive attitude toward Karolyn, my wife. My attitude is not based on her behavior but on my beliefs about who she is and about my role in her life.

Looking back on the various winter seasons of my marriage, I realize that my attitude during those times was not one of positive regard for Karolyn; instead, I focused on what I considered to be her weaknesses. Hurt or irritated by the things she said or left unsaid, annoyed by the things she did or failed to do, I found myself thinking the worst kind of thoughts about her and mentally blaming her for our poor relationship.

In my counseling practice, I have since discovered how common that destructive pattern of thinking is. One example is Marilyn from Kansas City, who has been married to Bruce for twenty-nine years. She indicated that she was definitely in a winter marriage. "I feel unloved and angry," she said.

"How did you arrive at this season of marriage?" I asked.

"We arrived here because of my husband's work. His job during parts of the year is demanding and requires lots of hours. So he is away from home most of the day. During these times, I become the head of the household, taking care of the boys and the finances. Also, he becomes distant and we don't have much communication. This has happened a lot during our twenty-nine years of marriage, and I would like to stop the cycle."

The good news is that Marilyn can stop the cycle. It begins by changing her attitude toward her husband. He is obviously a hardworking man, "bringing home the bacon." And by Marilyn's own testimony, he has never been sexually unfaithful to her. These are admirable traits. But Bruce has obviously not met Marilyn's emotional need for love and companionship. That is why she considers her marriage to be in the winter season.

Without realizing it, Marilyn has been sabotaging her marriage with a negative attitude. She has allowed the emotions of hurt, anger, and feelings of neglect to control her behavior toward Bruce. She has been verbally critical of him and the time he spends on the job, often saying such things as, "You let the company take advantage of you. You don't make any extra money for all the hours you invest. You ought to demand that they pay you more." On other occasions, she has focused on his neglect of the children: "How do you expect to have a positive influence on our boys when you don't spend any time with them?" The fact that Bruce played ball with the boys every Sunday afternoon and sometimes took them on business trips with him was overlooked in Marilyn's verbal tirades.

Bruce's attitude was also affected. "I don't ever do anything right," he said. "No matter what I do, it's never enough, so I've quit trying to please her. I tune her out when she gets into her long speeches. I just wish the boys didn't have to live in such a negative household." Bruce is also focusing on Marilyn's weaknesses and ignoring her strengths. The hours she spends tending to the household and helping the boys with homework are in the back of his mind, but what occupies his attention and guides his thinking are his focus on her angry lectures. All this could change if Bruce and Marilyn would choose a winning attitude. At the moment, they are continuing to perpetuate the winter season of marriage by their negative thinking toward each other.

BREAKING THE CYCLE OF NEGATIVITY

What is involved in choosing a winning attitude? First, we must acknowledge our negative thinking. Most of us tend to rationalize and excuse our negative attitudes. We say, "How do you expect me to react when they treat me like that?" Or, as one woman said while pointing her finger at her husband in my counseling office, "Yes, I have a negative attitude, and there's a reason for it. He's sitting right there."

As long as we rationalize our negative attitudes as legitimate, they will never change. If, however, we are tired of winter and would like to feel the hope of springtime again, we must recognize that our negative thinking must change. Our thinking guides our behavior. If we think negatively, we will behave in destructive ways. But if we think positively, our actions will be positive as well.

The second step toward a winning attitude is identifying your spouse's positive characteristics. I suggest that you make a written list. Ask God to bring to your mind all the positive things about your spouse, and then write them down. Enlist the help of your children by saying something like this: "I'm working on changing my attitude toward your father (or mother), and I'm trying to identify some of his positive traits. Would you tell me the things you like about your father, the things you appreciate and admire? I want to make a list." Not only will you get good feedback from your children, but you will also influence their thinking to turn in a positive direction. If your spouse has physically or verbally abused the children, you might preface your request by saying something like this: "I know that you feel hurt by your father in many ways. So do I. But I'm trying to change my attitude and give him credit for the positive contributions he makes to our lives. I need your help."

With help from God (and your kids), you will probably be able to make a fairly long list of your spouse's positive traits. However, even if the list is short, at least you have something positive on which to focus. One lady said about her husband, "I have to say he's a good whistler. It irritates me at times, but I've never heard anyone whistle better than he does. I guess he must have grown up with the song 'Whistle While You Work,' because that is what he does all the time."

The third step is to *focus* on those positive traits. Begin by thanking God for each one. If you are deeply hurt and want to recount to God your hurts before you give thanks, that's permissible. Your prayer might sound something like this. "Dear God, you know how my husband [or wife] treats me. You know the pain, hurt, and anger I feel. But I thank you that he [she] is not all bad. Here are the things for which I want to give thanks. I thank you that he [she] . . ."

Go through your list every day, thanking God for your spouse's positive characteristics. Ask God to turn your thinking toward the positive. Tell your spouse that you are tired of your negative, condemning messages toward him or her; acknowledge that those negative speeches have not helped the situation and that you intend to stop them.

A fourth step is to ask God to give you a biblical perspective of your spouse. Review the five characteristics of a Christian worldview listed on page 87 and begin to thank God for these five realities. Ask God to give you a new, positive attitude. Thank God that your spouse is made in the image of God and is therefore extremely valuable. Thank God that your spouse is uniquely gifted by God. Thank God that your spouse has a unique role to play in the Kingdom of God. Thank God that marriage was his idea, and acknowledge that he gave you your marriage as a blessing, not as a curse. Thank God that you have the opportunity to serve your spouse and to help your spouse accomplish more of his or her potential in the Kingdom of God.

Begin to express verbal appreciation to your spouse for the positive things that you see. Set a goal, such as one compliment a week for the first month, then two compliments per week for the second month, then three per week the third month, and so on until you work up to at least a compliment a day. In the wisdom literature of the Bible, we read these words: "The tongue has the power of life and death" (Proverbs 18:21). You can give your marriage new life when you begin to express verbal appreciation to your spouse. When you replace condemnation and criticism with words of affirmation, something inside your spouse will begin to warm toward you. In due time, he or she will begin to think of you in a more positive light, and more positive behavior will soon follow. This is not manipulation; it is simply the natural result of feeling appreciated.

BREAKING THE CYCLE OF NEGATIVITY

Acknowledge your negative thinking.

Identify and list your spouse's positive traits.

Teach yourself to focus on your spouse's positive traits.

Ask God to give you a biblical perspective of your spouse.

Express your appreciation verbally to your spouse.

I can hear some readers saying, "But what about my spouse's negative behavior? My attitude is not going to change that." Maybe not right away, but a positive attitude on your part will set in motion relational dynamics that create an atmosphere in which your spouse's behavior can change for the better. Simply stated, a positive attitude expressed in positive affirmations tends to create a positive response. The ice of winter begins to melt and the hope of spring is born. This is not deep psychology or profound theology. It is simply common sense. Choose a winning attitude and you are more likely to win. Tell yourself that you can be a better spouse and you will become one. Tell yourself that your spouse can make positive changes and he or she will. Tell yourself that, with God's help, you will see spring again and you are far more likely to see it.

Choosing a winning attitude works in all four seasons of marriage. If your marriage is in winter, it can start you on the road to spring. In a fall marriage, choosing to focus on your spouse's positive qualities can reopen the lines of communication and keep your marriage from fading into winter. In a spring or summer marriage, adopting a positive attitude will result in a further blossoming of your relationship and will help to establish a warmer climate in your marriage.

Another way to bring spring and summer to your marriage is described in Strategy 3.

STRATEGY 3

Learn to Speak Your Spouse's Love Language

I was standing in a grocery store checkout line one day when I glanced at the magazine rack. Of the twenty different magazines displayed there, seventeen had the word *love* at least once on the cover. Late one Saturday night, as I was driving home from the airport with my radio tuned to the local country station (there's nothing quite like country music to keep you awake when you are driving late at night), the DJ was playing "twelve in a row without commercial interruption." Of the twelve songs, ten focused on love.

If you watch the daytime soaps or prime-time TV or check the sales statistics on romance novels, you will have all the evidence you need that Western culture is obsessed with love. Yet, despite all the talk about love, the reality is that thousands of children go to bed every night feeling unloved by their parents, and thousands of husbands and wives go to bed feeling unloved by their spouse. Our culture is largely ignorant of the true nature of love and its effect on human relationships. Yet nothing holds more potential for changing the season of your marriage than learning the truth about love.

Part of the problem is that we use the word *love* rather loosely. Listen to any conversation on the street and you're likely to hear statements like these: "I love hot dogs." "I love the beach." "I love my baby." "I love the mountains." "I just love my new sports car." "I love my mother." "I love my dog." "I love the zoo." Is it any wonder, then, that when a husband says to his wife, "I love you, honey," she's not sure what to make of his statement?

In this chapter I'm not going to challenge our society's casual use of the word *love.* Instead, I'm going to focus on the importance of love as an essential human need. Whether we're educated or uneducated, we know instinctively that children need to feel loved. I like to describe each child as having an emotional love tank. When the love tank is full—that is, when the child genuinely feels loved by the parents—the child grows up normal and well adjusted. But when the love tank is empty, the child grows up with many internal struggles. During the teenage years, these children will go looking for love, typically in all the wrong places. Much misbehavior among children and teenagers stems from an empty love tank.

The same is true of adults. Married or single, every adult has an emotional love tank. When we feel loved by people significant to us, life is beautiful. When our love tank is empty, we struggle emotionally. Much misbehavior among adults grows out of an empty love tank.

For us married folks, the person we would most like to have love us is our spouse. If we feel loved by our spouse, the world looks bright. But if our love tank is empty, the world begins to look rather dark. Success in business, education, or sports will not satisfy the longing of the human heart for emotional love. When emotional love evaporates, marriages slip into fall and then winter. Conversely, when emotional love is rekindled, the warm breezes of spring and summer return to the marriage. In this chapter I want to focus on the nature of emotional love as it relates to marriage. What you are about to read has the potential to change the emotional climate of your marriage.

It all begins with "the tingles." In the normal course of life, we meet someone who catches our attention. There is something about the way he or she looks, talks, or acts that gives us a warm tingly feeling inside. The tingles are what motivate people to go out with each other. Sometimes, on the first date, we lose the tingles. We find out something intolerable about the other person and the tingles dissipate. But with some people, every time we get together, it just gets tinglier and tinglier. Eventually, we find ourselves emotionally obsessed. We're quite certain that he or she is the most wonderful person we've ever met. Everyone else will see the flaws, but we won't. Our parents may say, "Have you considered that he hasn't had a steady job in five years?" But we'll respond, "Give him a break. He's just waiting for the right opportunity." Our friends may ask, "Have you considered that she's been married five times before?" But we'll respond, "Those other guys were losers. The woman deserves to be happy, and I'm going to make her happy."

This stage of a romantic relationship can best be described as emotional obsession. We can't get the other person off our minds. We go to bed thinking about him, and we wake up thinking about him. All day long, we wonder what she's doing. Talking with her is the highlight of our day, and we want to spend as much time with her as possible. This obsession leads to irrational thoughts such as, *I'll never be happy unless we are together forever. Nothing else in life really matters.* In this stage of love, differences are minimized or denied. All we know is that we're happy, we've never been happier, and we intend to be happy for the rest of our lives.

This euphoric stage of love does not require a lot of effort. We are swept along by a river of positive emotions. We are willing to do almost anything for the benefit of the other person. It is during this time of emotional obsession that most people get married. They anticipate that they will continue to have these euphoric feelings for each other forever. They fail to understand that emotional obsession is only the initial stage of romantic love.

Research indicates that the average duration of this initial euphoria is two years.[1] When we come down off the emotional high, we must make the transition to the next stage of love, which is much more intentional and requires a conscious effort to meet the emotional needs of the other person. Many couples fail to make this transition. Instead, they get the tingles for someone else, divorce, and remarry, repeating the cycle with another mate. Sixty percent of those who remarry will experience a second divorce. And if perchance they try again, the divorce rate for third marriages is seventy-five percent.

The importance of learning how to make the transition from the obsessive stage to the intentional stage of love should be obvious. Just because we stay in a relationship does not mean that emotional love will continue to flow. The second stage of love is truly different from the first. The obsessive feelings we had for each other begin to fade, and we recognize other important pursuits in life besides pursuing each other. The illusions of perfection evaporate, and the words of our parents and friends return to our minds: "He hasn't had a steady job in five years." "She's been married five times before."

We start to wonder how we could have been so blind to reality. Differences in personality, interests, and lifestyle now become obvious, whereas before we hardly noticed. The euphoria that led us to put each other first and to focus on each other's well-being has now dissipated, and we begin to focus on ourselves and to realize that our spouse is no longer meeting our needs. We begin to request—and then demand—things from our mate, and when he or she refuses to meet our demands, we withdraw or lash out in anger. Our anger or withdrawal pushes our mate further away and makes it more difficult for him or her to express love to us.

Can such tarnished relationships be reborn? The answer is yes—if couples become aware of the nature of love and learn how to express love in a language their mate can understand. Good intentions are not enough. We must also learn how to meet our spouse's emotional need for love. People are different. What makes one person feel loved will not necessarily make another person feel loved. By nature, we tend to express love to others in the way we wish they would express love to us. When our spouse doesn't respond positively to our expressions of love, we get frustrated. The problem is not the sincerity of our love; the problem is that we are speaking the wrong love language. If we speak our own love language but not our mate's, we will fail to communicate.

I am often asked to explain the popularity of my book *The Five Love Languages,* which has now sold more than three million copies and has been translated into thirty-four languages around the world. I believe that the book has been successful because it has helped people learn to make the transition from obsessive love to intentional love; it has taught people how to discover and speak their spouse's love language and thus keep emotional love alive in their relationship. In the remainder of this chapter, I want to give you a brief summary of the five love languages. Regardless of which season your marriage is now in, learning to speak your partner's love language will enhance your communication, fill your spouse's love tank, and strengthen your relationship. If your marriage is in fall or winter, learning to speak your spouse's love language may be the key to turning your marriage around and heading forward into spring and summer.

THE FIVE LOVE LANGUAGES

After thirty years as a marriage counselor, I am convinced that there are five basic love languages—five ways to express love emotionally. Each person has a primary love language that we must learn to speak if we want a person to feel loved.[2]

Words of Affirmation

One time when my wife and I were visiting our daughter and son-in-law and our two grandchildren, our son-in-law took the garbage out after dinner. When he walked back into the room where we were talking with our daughter, she looked up and said, "John, thanks for taking the garbage out." Inside I said, "*Yes!*" because I knew the power of appreciation. I can't tell you how many men and women have sat in my office over the past thirty years and said to me, "I work my tail off every day, yet my spouse acts like I haven't done a thing. I never get a single word of appreciation." If your spouse's primary love language is words of affirmation, your spoken praise and appreciation will fall like rain on parched soil. Before long, you will see new life sprouting in your marriage as your spouse responds to your words of love.

Acts of Service

Do you remember the old saying, "Actions speak louder than words"? For some people, that is particularly true of love. If acts of service is your spouse's primary love language, nothing will speak more deeply to him or her emotionally than simple acts of service. Maxine, who had been married for fifteen years, came to my office one day because she was frustrated with her marriage. Listen to what she said: "I don't understand David. Every day he tells me that he loves me, but he never does anything to help me. He just sits on the couch watching TV while I wash the dishes, and the thought never crosses his mind to help me. I'm sick of hearing 'I love you.' If he loved me, he would do something to help me."

Maxine's primary love language is acts of service (not words of affirmation), and even though her husband, David, loved her, he had never learned to express his love in a way that made her *feel* loved. However, after David and I talked and he read *The Five Love Languages,* he got the picture and started speaking Maxine's love language. In less than a month, her love tank was beginning to fill up, and their marriage moved from winter to spring. The next time I talked to Maxine, she said, "It's wonderful. I wish we had come for counseling ten years ago. I never knew about the love languages. I just knew I didn't feel loved."

101

Receiving Gifts

In every society throughout human history, gift giving has been perceived as an expression of love. Giving gifts is universal, because there is something inside the human psyche that says if you love someone, you will give to him or her. What many people do not understand is that for some people, receiving gifts is their primary love language. It's the thing that makes them feel loved most deeply. If you're married to someone whose primary love language is gift giving, you will make your spouse feel loved and treasured by giving gifts on birthdays, holidays, anniversaries, and "no occasion" days. The gifts need not be expensive or elaborate; it's the thought that counts. Even something as simple as a homemade card or a few cheerful flowers will communicate your love to your spouse. Little things mean a lot to a person whose primary love language is receiving gifts.

Quality Time

If your spouse's love language is quality time, giving him or her your undivided attention is one of the best ways you can show your love. Some men pride themselves on being able to watch television, read a magazine, and listen to their wives, all at the same time. That is an admirable trait, but it is not speaking the love language of quality time. Instead, you must turn off the TV, lay the magazine down, look into your mate's eyes, and *listen* and *interact*. To your spouse, twenty minutes of your undivided attention—listening and conversing—is like a twenty-minute refill of his or her love tank.

Men, if you really want to impress your wife, the next time she walks into the room while you are watching a sporting event, put the television on mute and don't take your eyes off her as long as she's in the room. If she engages you in conversation, turn the TV off and give her your undivided attention. You will score a thousand points and her love tank will be overflowing.

Physical Touch

We have long known the emotional power of physical touch. That's why we pick up babies and touch them tenderly. Long before an infant understands the meaning of the word *love,* he or she *feels* loved by physical touch. In marriage, the love language of physical touch includes everything from putting a hand on your mate's shoulder as you walk by, touching his or her leg as you're driving together, and holding hands while you're walking to kissing, embracing, and sexual intercourse. If physical touch is your spouse's primary love language, nothing communicates love more clearly than for you to take the initiative to reach out and touch your mate.

DISCOVERING YOUR SPOUSE'S LOVE LANGUAGE

If the key to meeting your spouse's need for emotional love is learning to speak his or her love language, how can you discover what that love language is? It's simple. Listen to your spouse's complaints. Here are five common complaints and the love language that each reveals:

"You mean you didn't bring me anything? Did you even miss me while you were gone?" (receiving gifts)

"We never spend any time with each other anymore. We're like two ships passing in the dark." (quality time)

"I don't think you would ever touch me if I didn't initiate it." (physical touch)

"I can't do anything right around here. All you ever do is criticize. I can never please you." (words of affirmation)

"If you loved me, you would *do* something around here. You never lift a finger to help." (acts of service)

Typically, when our spouse complains, we get irritated. But he or she is actually giving us valuable information. Complaints often reveal the key to our spouse's inner longing for emotional love. If we learn our mate's primary love language—and speak it—we will have a happier spouse and a better marriage.

But what if your spouse's primary love language is something that isn't easy for you to do? What if you're not a touchy-feely person but your spouse's primary love language is physical touch? The answer is simple, though not necessarily *easy:* You learn to speak the language of physical touch. You learn to speak a new love language by *trying.* At first it might be very difficult, but the second time will be easier, and the third time even easier. Eventually, you can become proficient in speaking your mate's love language; and if he or she reciprocates by speaking your language, the two of you will keep emotional love alive in your marriage forever.

My files are filled with letters from people who tell me that learning their spouse's primary love language revolutionized their marriage. For example, Rick, a thirty-three-year-old truck driver who has been married for twelve years, wrote, "We have the best marriage we've ever had. My wife purchased *The Five Love Languages* on audiotape for me so I could listen in my tractor trailer. We were in a winter season at this stage in our marriage. After I discovered her love language, it helped me to understand why she had been saying that I didn't love her. I knew I loved her, and I told her all the time. The problem was that her love language is acts of service, and I never did anything to help her around the house. I guess I followed my dad's example—but then Mom and Dad never had a very good marriage, either. Now I try to do things for Brenda when I'm home. It has made a great difference in our marriage."

Rick's wife, Brenda, wrote, "We were having serious problems and were talking about separating. I had a friend who let me read her copy of *The Five Love Languages.* Then Rick and I started talking about our relationship. I learned that his love language is words of affirmation. Here I had been criticizing him because I didn't feel loved by him, but all along I was only making him feel worse and didn't know it. Now he speaks my language and I speak his. We went from a very wintry season to a warm spring or summer season." Understanding your spouse's primary love language—and learning to speak it—can make a world of difference in your marriage.

What if your spouse is unwilling to read a book about marriage or discuss your marriage? With marriages in the fall and winter seasons, this is often the case. One spouse becomes concerned enough about the marriage to read a book, attend a seminar, or go for counseling, while the other spouse is unwilling to do anything. This is when unconditional love becomes exceedingly important. It is easy to love your spouse when your spouse is loving you. It is easy to say kind words to your spouse when he or she is treating you kindly. But even if your spouse is unwilling to try or to reciprocate, unconditional love means that you will *choose* to love your spouse in his or her primary love language.

105

Although unconditional love is difficult, it is the kind of love that God has for us. Romans 5:8 says that God loved us "while we were still sinners" and sent Christ to die for us. Scripture also says that we love God "because he first loved us" (1 John 4:19). Therefore, when you choose to love your spouse unconditionally, you are following God's example. And if you ask God, he will give you the ability to do it.

In Romans 5:5 the apostle Paul says, "God has poured out his love into our hearts by the Holy Spirit." Likewise, when you pour out your love by speaking your spouse's love language, you are doing the most emotionally powerful thing you can do. Your spouse desperately needs emotional love from you. As your spouse's love tank begins to fill, there is a good chance that he or she will begin to reciprocate. A full love tank creates a positive atmosphere in which you and your spouse can talk about your differences more easily and negotiate solutions to your conflicts. I have seen many hard, cold men and women melt when they begin to receive love in their love language. Love is the most powerful weapon in the world for good. It can thaw the coldest of winters and bring the blossoms of spring to your marriage.

STRATEGY 4

Develop the Awesome Power of Empathetic Listening

The ability to speak and the ability to listen are two of the more profound gifts that God has given to humanity. Animals don't sit around the campfire reminiscing about what happened five years ago or discussing what they hope will happen in the future. But people do. Oral communication is the foundation of all human culture. These abilities to speak and to listen allow us to pass ideas from one mind to another.

Likewise, in a marriage nothing is more fundamental than talking and listening. This simple transaction is the vehicle that allows couples to process life together as teammates. Open communication is the lifeblood that keeps a marriage in the spring and summer seasons. Conversely, failure to communicate is what brings on fall and winter.

Speaking and listening—it sounds so simple. So why is it that when divorced individuals were asked in a survey, "Why did your marriage fail?" eighty-seven percent said, "Deficient communication"?

Could these marriages have been redeemed and restored? I believe the answer is yes—if the couples had learned some positive communication patterns. The key to improving communication with one's spouse lies in developing the power of empathetic listening. Empathy means to enter into another person's world, to seek to walk in his or her shoes and see the world from his or her perspective. An empathetic husband seeks to understand what his wife is experiencing—her thoughts, feelings, and desires. And the same is true of an empathetic wife toward her husband. She seeks to understand his dreams, his hopes, his fears. Empathetic listening encourages other people to talk, because they know they will be heard.

Unfortunately, by nature we tend to be judgmental listeners. We evaluate what the other person says based on our own view of the situation, and we respond by pronouncing our judgment. Judgmental listening tends to stop the flow of communication— and we wonder why our spouse doesn't talk more! By failing at the art of empathetic listening, we sabotage intimacy, the very thing we so desperately want.

The goal of this chapter is to help you learn how to promote positive communication by means of empathetic listening. This may require a radical change in the way you converse with your spouse. It will certainly take effort and practice, but the rewards will be overwhelmingly positive. For most of us, empathetic listening requires a significant change of attitude. We must shift from *egocentric* listening (viewing the conversation through our own eyes) to *empathetic* listening (viewing the conversation through our spouse's eyes). The goal of empathetic listening is to see the world from your spouse's perspective and thus understand what he or she is experiencing inside—both *perceptions* and *feelings*. This is important: You will never understand your spouse if you limit your listening to perceptions, thoughts, opinions, and desires. You must also understand the *feelings* that lie behind the thoughts.

The husband who says, "I think I'll just stop going to church" and the wife who responds, "Why would you do that? That's not going to help anything" have had a brief dialogue, but little understanding. On the other hand, if the wife responds, "What makes you say that?" and the husband says, "I just get so discouraged hearing the same old condemning sermons every Sunday," they are now on the road to understanding. If they continue this process of empathetic listening, they may well come to understand each other.

Perhaps you're thinking, *I would be happy to listen to my spouse and to try to understand, if only he or she would say something.* If your spouse is noncommunicative, I can guarantee there's a reason—or reasons—for the silence. Perhaps your husband was not encouraged to talk as a child. Maybe his ideas were discounted or ignored by his parents until he developed the attitude, "Why talk? No one's listening." Maybe your wife has tried to communicate her thoughts and opinions but has felt put down or condemned. Thus, she reasons, *Who wants to be rejected? It's easier just to keep my mouth shut.*

On the other hand, it may simply be a matter of personality. In my counseling practice, I have identified two distinct personality types when it comes to talking: Dead Sea people and Babbling Brooks. With a Dead Sea personality, information flows in, but nothing ever comes back out. Just like the Dead Sea in Israel, which has no outlet but only receives and stores water from the Jordan River, Dead Sea personalities receive thoughts, feelings, and experiences throughout the day—and they are perfectly content not to talk about them. If you ask these people, "What's wrong? Why aren't you talking?" their typical response will be, "Nothing's wrong. What makes you think something's wrong?" To a Dead Sea personality, it is perfectly natural not to talk.

The contrasting personality type is the Babbling Brook. Whatever they see or hear, they talk about. If no one is home to listen, they will call someone on the telephone and say, "Do you know what I just saw?" "Do you know what I just heard?" They have no reservoir.

Usually these two personalities marry each other. Babbling Brooks are attracted to Dead Seas because they are such wonderful listeners. Dead Seas are comfortable with Babbling Brooks because they are not pressured to talk. The good news is that a Dead Sea can learn to talk and a Babbling Brook can learn to "slow the flow." Effective communication is a choice.

Empathetic listening will encourage a Dead Sea spouse to talk because it creates an atmosphere of genuine interest in what he or she is saying. If negative feelings have developed because of past treatment in childhood or in the marriage, empathetic listening tends to bring healing. In fact, the quickest way to deal constructively with negative feelings is to make the person feel heard and understood.

Another question I am commonly asked is, "How can I listen empathetically when my spouse's words are critical and harsh?" Again, the answer lies in understanding what is behind the harsh, critical words. Typically, a spouse who speaks critically speaks out of a heart filled with hurt and anger from past mistreatment. We're all human, and we tend to get defensive when our self-esteem is threatened. But because empathetic listening incorporates both feelings and perceptions, it is the most effective means of helping people to process their hurt and anger—which is why it is one of the primary skills of an effective counselor. I am not suggesting that you become a counselor to your spouse. But I am suggesting that if you learn the art of empathetic listening, you can be part of the solution rather than part of the problem.

Empathetic listening is also an effective vehicle for building your mate's self-esteem. When your spouse has a healthy self-esteem, he or she will be less defensive.

Even if your spouse has some dysfunctional patterns of communication, empathetic listening can potentially create a climate where those patterns can be discovered and changed. Judgmental listening, on the other hand, simply perpetuates the problem. That's why many couples come to the point of saying, "We simply can't communicate, so why try?" Fall turns to winter, and winter often ends in divorce. I repeat my conviction that many of these divorces could have been averted if at least one of the spouses had learned the awesome power of empathetic listening.

LEARNING TO LISTEN EMPATHETICALLY

Empathetic listeners approach every conversation with the attitude of trying to understand the other person. "I want to know what is going on in my spouse's mind and heart." "I want to enter into his or her joys and sorrows." Such levels of understanding are essential if you want to have an intimate marriage.

One of the characteristics of empathetic listening is developing a *genuine attitude of understanding.* This is no small matter, nor will it be easy for most of us. Psychologist Paul Tournier expressed it well when he said, "Each one speaks primarily in order to set forth his own ideas. . . . Exceedingly few exchanges of viewpoints manifest a real desire to understand the other person."[1]

By nature we are all egocentric. The world revolves around *me.* The way *I* think and feel is the most important issue. It is a giant step in maturity when we choose to develop an attitude of empathy—honestly seeking to understand the thoughts and feelings of another person. The apostle Peter challenges men in particular when he writes to husbands, "Be considerate as you live with your wives, and treat them with respect" (1 Peter 3:7). According to Proverbs 18:2, egocentric living is foolish: "A fool finds no pleasure in understanding but delights in airing his own opinions." Thus, when we ask God to help us change our attitudes, to give us a genuine desire to understand our spouse, we are showing signs of wisdom.

Another important aspect of empathetic listening is *choosing to withhold judgment* on our spouse's ideas. Here again we may need to radically shift our way of thinking. After all, we have opinions on just about everything, and we're convinced that our perspective is accurate. Otherwise, we'd change our views, right? But when we say, "The way I see the situation is the way it is," we fail to recognize that our spouse thinks the same thing about his or her own opinions. Because we are both egocentric, we often have differing opinions about the same situation. That is simply part of being human and being married. Spouses often see things very differently.

If I listen to my wife with a view to "setting her straight," I will never understand her, and most of our conversations will end in arguments with no resolution, leaving us as enemies rather than friends, opponents rather than teammates.

It is this propensity to pass judgment that daily sabotages the conversations of thousands of couples. When a wife says, "I think I am going to have to quit my job," and the husband responds, "You can't quit your job. We can't make it without your salary. And remember you're the one who wanted this house," they are either on the road to an intense argument or else they will withdraw and suffer in silence, each blaming the other for the coldness of winter that settles on their marriage. But how very different the conversation would be if the husband withheld judgment and instead responded to his wife by saying, "It sounds like you had a hard day at work, honey. Do you want to talk about it?" He has now opened up the possibility of understanding his wife. And when she feels understood, together they can make a wise decision regarding her job. It is the withholding of judgment that allows the conversation to proceed.

A third characteristic of empathetic listening is the most important but also the most difficult: *Affirm your spouse even when you disagree with his or her ideas.* How do you do this? By affirming your spouse for sharing his or her ideas and feelings with you. In other words, you express your appreciation to your spouse for being open and honest with you.

Affirmation is a big step beyond merely withholding judgment. When you affirm your spouse verbally, you give him or her the freedom to have ideas that differ from your own and to have feelings that you would not have in a similar situation.

113

Your affirmation might be verbalized in statements similar to these: "I appreciate that you are sharing your ideas and feelings with me. Now I can understand why you could feel so hurt. If I were in your shoes, I'm sure I would feel the same way. I want you to know that I love you very much, and it hurts me to see you hurting, but at least now I understand what's going on inside you. And I appreciate your being open with me. Obviously all of this affects me, and I have some thoughts and feelings about it. I'm not sure I can verbalize them, but I would be willing to try whenever you want to hear them. But please know that I am with you. I love you, and I want to do whatever I can to help."

A partner who hears these affirming words may or may not be ready immediately to receive the spouse's perspective. But he or she will feel understood and affirmed. Nothing is more important than affirmation to create an atmosphere in which one spouse will eventually be willing to hear the other's perspective.

Developing the art of affirmation, whether you agree or disagree with your spouse's ideas, creates a positive climate that encourages your mate to share openly, and it cultivates the soil in which the seeds of teamwork can be planted. Eventually, those seeds will blossom into the flowers of spring and summer.

The capstone of empathetic listening is that you *share your own ideas only when your spouse feels understood*. As with the other steps, this one may require a monumental change in our typical communication patterns. By nature, we are quick to give our ideas. In fact, one research project indicates that the average person listens for seventeen seconds before interrupting to give his or her own ideas on the subject. That is egocentric listening at its worst and seldom results in productive conversation. Empathetic listening, on the other hand, creates a positive climate in which your spouse will almost certainly want to hear what you have to say.

When your mate feels understood rather than condemned, he or she will be far more open to hearing your point of view. Empathetic listening stimulates positive feelings. The most common mistake in most marital conversations is the premature expres-

---

THE FOUR KEYS OF EMPATHETIC LISTENING

Listen with an attitude of understanding (not judgment).

Withhold judgment on your spouse's ideas.

Affirm your spouse, even when you disagree with his or her ideas.

Share your own ideas only when your spouse feels understood.

sion of ideas. Such behavior almost always ends in unproductive arguments that leave the couple more estranged and the marriage that much closer to winter.

Marissa came to my marriage seminar alone. She described her marriage in the following way: "Our marriage is no fun. We are definitely in the winter season. I don't want to go home at night and deal with my husband. I want things to change. I know that we both must change. I tend to shut him out. I don't talk to him. When we try talking, we argue about everything. I don't listen to him, and he doesn't listen to me. I talked to him on the phone last night after our session, and he is open to reading a book with me. I hope that our marriage can get better." I had the sense that if Marissa could learn the skills of empathetic listening, she could turn her marriage toward spring. What are the practical skills that can help Marissa—and you—develop the art of empathetic listening?

LEARNING THE SKILLS OF EMPATHETIC LISTENING

The ideas I am going to share are not mysterious. They are not wrapped in psychological terms. But even though they are easy to understand, mastering them will take conscious effort and practice. I believe that anyone who sincerely tries can learn the awesome power of empathetic listening. I suggest that you read the following list of ideas again and again until they become a part of your thinking. When your spouse starts talking to you, ask God to help you remember and apply the skills that will be most meaningful to your spouse. Daily pray the prayer of St. Francis of Assisi, who prayed, "O Divine Master, grant that I may not so much seek to . . . be understood as to understand." That is a prayer that God will answer. Put the following steps into practice (and you *will* have to practice!) and watch your communication blossom:

115

1. *Listen with your eyes.* Give your spouse your undivided attention. Turn off the TV. Put down the book or magazine and look at your spouse. Eye contact communicates, "What you are saying is important to me."

2. *Listen with your mouth.* Keep it closed for at least five minutes. Interjecting your ideas too soon indicates that you are not in an empathetic listening mode. As long as your spouse is talking, your role is to listen. Remember, your goal is to find out what is going on in your spouse's mind and heart.

3. *Listen with your neck.* Nodding your head indicates, "I'm trying to understand what you are saying. I'm with you."

4. *Listen with your hands.* Don't fidget with a pencil, paper, or the TV remote control. Let your hands relax at your sides or on your legs. Don't put them behind your neck or stretch to the ceiling as if you are bored.

5. *Listen with your back.* Lean forward occasionally while your spouse is talking, rather than sitting rigidly. A slight forward movement of the body communicates, "You have my full attention."

6. *Listen with your feet.* Stay put. Don't walk out of the room while your spouse is talking—unless, of course, an emergency erupts in the next room. If that happens, tell your spouse why you are leaving. For example, "Honey, let me put out this fire in the kitchen and I'll be right back."

7. *Listen for feelings as well as for facts.* If you only listen and respond to what your spouse says—and ignore feelings—he or she will not feel understood.

8. *As you listen, try to see the situation from your spouse's perspective.* Try to understand your spouse's interpretation of the situation and his or her feelings about what has

happened. This is difficult to do, because we humans are naturally egocentric, but it is essential if you are to become an empathetic listener.

⑨ *Resist the urge to share your perspective before your spouse feels understood.* Don't tell your spouse that he or she doesn't have the facts straight, is misunderstanding your intentions, or has no right to feel angry or disappointed. Never share your perspective until you understand your spouse's perspective. Once your mate feels understood , he or she will be far more likely, and far better able, to listen to your opinion.

⑩ *Seek to clarify your understanding of your spouse's ideas by asking reflective questions.* "What I hear you saying is that you think _____. Am I understanding you correctly?" When your spouse responds to your question, nod affirmingly. Don't jump into "battle mode" even if you disagree with what your spouse is saying.

⑪ *Seek to clarify your understanding of your spouse's emotions by asking reflective questions.* "It seems to me that you are feeling disappointed because _____. Is that correct?" Your spouse may agree or may say, "Disappointed? How about hurt, angry, and frustrated!" Again, an affirming nod from you will communicate, "I'm hearing you."

⑫ *Summarize your understanding of your mate's thoughts and feelings.* "What I am understanding you to say is that you are hurt and angry because you feel that I let you down by not _____. Is that correct?" When your spouse indicates that you understand what he or she is thinking and feeling, you are now ready for the most important step in empathetic listening: affirmation.

⑬ *Affirm your spouse's thoughts and feelings verbally.* You might say something like this: "As I listen to you, I can see how you would feel hurt and angry at me. If I were in your shoes, I'm sure I would feel the same way." (And you would if you were truly seeing the situation from your spouse's perspective.) Verbal affirmation of your spouse's thoughts and feelings is what makes you an understanding mate rather than an enemy.

⑭ *Request permission to share your perspective.* Now that you have fully heard your spouse and understand his or her thoughts and feelings, you are ready to ask permission to share your own perspective. You might say something like this: "I really appreciate your sharing with me. Now I understand why you would be upset [or whatever emotion you sense he or she is feeling]. Can I share with you my perspective, because I think it will let you know what was going on inside me through all this?" If your spouse is open—and people typically are open after they feel understood—you are now free to share your perspective of what you did and why you did it.

By listening empathetically to your spouse, you create an atmosphere in which your spouse is more likely to listen empathetically to you. When two people are seeking to understand each other, usually they will. Then they can seek a solution to their problem. When they seek to resolve—rather than win—an argument, they not only discover workable solutions but also find intimacy with their spouse. Few things are more important in moving a marriage from fall or winter back to spring or summer than the awesome power of empathetic listening.

STRATEGY 5

*Discover the Joy of Helping
Your Spouse Succeed*

What is success? Ask a dozen people and you may get a dozen different answers. A friend of mine said, "Success is making the most of who you are with what you've got." I like that definition. Every person has the potential to make a positive impact on the world. It all depends on what we do with what we have. Success is measured not by the amount of money we possess or the position we attain but by how we use our resources and our opportunities. Position and money can be used to help others, or they can be squandered or abused. The truly successful people are those who help others succeed.

The same is true in marriage. A successful wife is one who expends her time and energy helping her husband reach his potential for God and for doing good in the world. Likewise, a successful husband is one who helps his wife succeed. An old adage says, "You can't help a man uphill without getting closer to the top yourself." I agree with my friend Harold Sala, who said, "With the possible exception of the parents who give a son guidance in the early years of his life, no single person contributes to the success of a man more than his wife."[1] It could also be said that a husband makes the greatest contribution to his wife's success (or failure).

I must confess that I knew very little about helping my wife succeed in the early days of our marriage. I suppose that in a general sense I wanted her to be happy and successful. But the main focus of my attention was on what she could do for *me.* When she did not live up to my expectations, I sought to motivate her by manipulation. My theme was, "I would treat you better if you would treat me better." It took me several years to discover the joy of helping Karolyn succeed, but when I did, our marriage went from winter to spring in a few short weeks.

So, how does one get started? For me, it began with a fresh examination of the life and teachings of Jesus Christ. Few people would deny that Jesus has had the most positive impact on human history of any man who ever lived. Yet his approach was not manipulative or self-serving. In fact, quite the contrary: He led by serving others. During the three-and-a-half years of his public life, he healed the sick, fed the hungry, spoke with kindness to the downtrodden, and brought hope to the destitute. The apostle Peter summarized the life of Jesus with this statement: "He went around doing good."[2]

Perhaps Jesus' greatest act of service—apart from his sacrificial death on our behalf—was when he took a basin of water and a towel and performed the lowly task of washing his disciples' feet. With that simple yet profound act of service—doing what needed to be done but what no one else wanted to do—Jesus demonstrated humility, love, and true leadership.

Husbands, are you willing to humble yourself to such a degree to serve your wife? Wives, are you willing to serve your husband in such a way? Jesus removed all doubt about his intentions when he said, "Now that I, your Lord and Teacher, have washed your feet, you also should wash one another's feet. I have set you an example that you should do as I have done for you. . . . Now that you know these things, you will be blessed if you do them."[3] On another occasion Jesus told his followers, "Whoever wants to become great among you must be your servant."[4] It's a great paradox—the way up is down. True greatness is expressed through serving, not by seeking one's own agenda.

This principle is true in marriage as well as in all of life. A truly great husband is one who is willing to serve his wife. A truly great wife is one who is willing to serve her husband. If you want to breathe new life into a fall or winter marriage, start serving your spouse. If your marriage is in spring or summer and you want to keep it there, start serving your spouse. Mowing the grass, cooking meals, cleaning the bathroom, vacuuming floors, doing the laundry, taking care of the kids while your spouse goes to the gym, washing the car, trimming the shrubs, helping with a computer problem, and cleaning out the garage are all examples of acts of service. It took me a long time to figure out that life's greatest meaning is found in *giving,* not in *getting.* When I finally grasped this profound principle, it made a significant difference in my marriage.

For me, this attitude of service required an acute change of heart. My egocentric spirit had to be released, not to my wife but to God. I remember the day I prayed a simple prayer: "Lord, give me the attitude of Christ. I want to serve my wife as Jesus served his followers." As I look back on four decades of marriage, I'm convinced that God's answer to *that* prayer had a greater impact on my marriage than any prayer I have ever prayed.

Once your heart attitude is changed, it is simply a matter of learning how to express service in ways that will help your spouse reach his or her potential for good. Three simple questions made this practical for me. When I was willing to ask Karolyn these three questions (and do what she suggested!), I was on the road to helping her become successful. The questions are: (1) What can I do to help you? (2) How can I make your life easier? and (3) How can I be a better husband? My wife's responses to these three questions gave me the agenda that changed our marriage forever.

THREE SIMPLE QUESTIONS TO HELP YOUR SPOUSE SUCCEED

1. What can I do to help you?

2. How can I make your life easier?

3. How can I be a better husband (wife)?

If you are in the winter season of marriage and are afraid that if you ask those questions, your spouse will simply say, "It's too late. I don't want to hear that," let me suggest a different approach: Reflect on the complaints your spouse has made during your marriage. Those complaints reveal his or her hidden desires. You may have found them annoying at the time, but now that you have an attitude of service, they give you valuable information. Simply begin doing and saying the things your spouse has requested through the years, and you may well see a softening in his or her attitude. Ultimately, it is difficult to reject a husband or wife who is sincerely trying to help you succeed.

Many couples have shared with me their experience in discovering this strategy. I met Phil in Birmingham, Alabama. He was thirty-seven and had been married to his second wife for two years. He said, "We have gone from fall to spring. I have had to learn to change things about myself that will make our marriage better. I have to continually discover what's important to my wife and try to give it to her. I'm transitioning into more communication, which is hard for me. I had put sports and tailgating with friends over her for a period of time. I also didn't talk to her at all, and instead I shared things with others that should have been kept between the two of us. When I started spending quality time with her and started doing things that mattered to her, her attitude changed."

Darlene, whom I met in Denver, was forty-eight and had been married to Rod for thirty years. "One major thing that made a difference," she said, "was that I began to understand more about my husband's needs. I was in 'mother mode' most of the time and tended to forget that I was a wife, too, and that my husband needed me as much as my children did. I now realize that he is the one I will be spending my whole life with, not our children or our parents. Understanding the five love languages was so exciting to me and helped open me up to things my husband needs. I am continuing to learn to speak words of affirmation, which I know he needs. My husband has learned that I need him to spend more time with me and I need his help in doing things for me. He has learned how to talk with me more. With his compliments and patience, I have become a much happier person. We have definitely moved from winter to spring in our marriage." Darlene and Rod have discovered the joy of helping each other succeed.

What are some practical ways you could help your spouse succeed? The best answer to that question will come from him or her, but let me share with you some of the things that other couples have found to be extremely helpful.

One of the most effective ways to help your spouse is to *offer encouraging words.* The word *encourage* means "to inspire courage." All of us have areas in which we feel insecure and lack courage, and that lack of courage often hinders us from accomplishing the positive things that we would like to do. The latent potential within your spouse may await your encouraging words.

A couple who were being interviewed on the occasion of their fiftieth wedding anniversary were asked, "To what do you attribute the success of your long marriage?" The husband responded, "Sarah was the first young lady I ever dated. When I proposed to her, I was scared stiff. But after the wedding, her dad took me aside and handed me a little package and said, 'Here is all you really need to know.'"

The obvious question was, "And what was in that package?"

Reaching into his pocket, the man pulled out a gold watch and said, "This is it." There across the face of the watch, where he could see it a dozen times a day, was written, *Say something nice to Sarah.* "That," he said, "is the key to our marriage."[5]

Life can sometimes be difficult, but when we receive positive words, we are encouraged to continue pursuing our dreams. When a man fails to get a promotion at work, he may feel that he is a failure. But when his wife says, "You're still number one in my book," he has the courage to work through his disappointment and continue.

I was speaking at a church in Spokane, Washington, when I first heard Julia sing. After the service, I commended her for the excellent way she sang. "I'll have to give my husband credit for that," she said.

"How's that?" I asked.

"Six years ago, I expressed the desire to take voice lessons. It's something I have always wanted to do. We had been married four years and had two preschool children. When I shared the idea with my husband, he said, 'Go for it. I'll be glad to keep the children. You have such a beautiful voice; you need to develop the talent God has given you.'"

"That's quite a husband you have," I said.

"He's the absolute greatest," Julia responded.

Perhaps your spouse has untapped potential in one or more areas of life. That potential may be awaiting your encouraging words. Perhaps your wife needs to enroll in a course to develop her potential. Maybe your husband needs to meet some people who have succeeded in his area of interest who can give him insight on the next step to take. Your words may supply the necessary courage to take that first step. Most of us have more potential than we will ever develop. What holds us back is often lack of courage. A loving spouse can supply that all-important catalyst.

125

Julia's husband not only gave her encouraging words, he also took supportive action, which is a second way of helping your spouse to succeed. He was not only willing to keep the children once a week while Julia took voice lessons, he was also willing to use the family finances to help her accomplish her dream. One of the most common complaints I have encountered in my counseling office has been the husbands and wives who say "My spouse is not supportive." They sometimes add, "I feel like he [she] works against me rather than for me."

Now, I must admit that sometimes this "lack of support" is another way of saying, "My spouse will not go along with all my crazy ideas." There are people who are dreamers but never attach their dreams to reality. They jump into a business venture and lose thousands of dollars, then can't understand why their spouse is not ready to jump into the next venture with them.

There are, however, ways of being supportive even if your mate is an unrealistic dreamer. I'm not suggesting that you blindly support your spouse in an endeavor that you think is destined for failure. However, you might say something like this: "More than anything, I want to see you succeed in life. I'm encouraged that you have dreams. At the same time, I don't want to see you fail again. Therefore, I'm going to be very supportive of you in this idea, but I'm going to request that you talk with a banker or someone who could give you good information about this venture before you jump into it. I know that if you continue to try business ventures that fail, you will eventually get discouraged. I don't want that to happen. I want you to succeed, so let's get all the wisdom we can up front. Then let's jump together or let's decide not to jump at all." In such a statement, you are expressing your desire to be supportive in the most responsible manner.

Often supportive actions spell the difference between success and failure. When your wife expresses a desire to join a weight-loss program, don't say what one husband said: "We can't afford that. Why don't you just stop eating?" Such a nonsupportive attitude not only sabotaged her dream but also the marriage. Helping your spouse succeed requires time, energy, effort, and perhaps sacrifice on your part.

I am forever indebted to my wife for supporting me when I went back to graduate school. She took care of our young daughter while I worked part time and went to school. We lived on a shoestring. For three years, she never bought a pair of shoes or a new dress for herself. Her sacrificial actions made it possible for me to complete graduate school. I would like to think that whatever success I have experienced brings her a great deal of satisfaction, knowing that she is largely responsible for my successes. By the way, she now has plenty of shoes and dresses.

What desires has your spouse expressed? What supportive actions would it require on your part to see those dreams become realities? Why not express your willingness to support your spouse, both with encouragement and with supportive action? Few things give greater joy than seeing your spouse reach his or her potential for God and for good.

FOUR PRACTICAL WAYS TO HELP YOUR SPOUSE SUCCEED

1. Offer encouraging words.

2. Take supportive action.

3. Provide emotional support.

4. Express respect for your spouse.

I recently met a husband whose wife is a public speaker. He said, "I gave up my job so I could travel with her. I take care of her books and tapes and luggage. My greatest joy is in seeing her do what she enjoys most. I feel that by serving her, I am serving God." Here is a husband who has discovered the joy of helping his spouse succeed.

A third practical way to help your spouse succeed is by giving emotional support. Emotions—positive and negative—are gifts from God. How dull life would be if we were not able to feel. Try to imagine watching a sunset, a ball game, or the ocean and feeling no emotion. We would be something less than human if we had no feelings. We are made in the image of God, and part of what that means is that we are emotional creatures.

Unlike thoughts, which ideally we can control, our emotions are not nearly as manageable. Feelings are unsolicited, interior, personal reactions to what goes on around us or to what has happened to us in the past. Feelings are as common as breathing, yet many people talk about feelings as enemies. We sometimes hear people say such things as, "My emotions are about to destroy me."

Why do we pit ourselves against our emotions? One reason is that we have seen so many other people who have followed their emotions and reaped destruction. They have done what they felt like doing and everyone around them suffered.

Another reason we don't trust our feelings is that we know they change. They lift us up, and they let us down. Our highs don't last, and our lows seem to drag on forever. We conclude, therefore, that emotions are unreliable and that we must live independent of them if we are to have success. Perhaps the chief reason we consider emotions our enemies is that negative emotions don't seem to fit in with being "a joyful Christian." Anger, fear, disappointment, loneliness, frustration, depression, and sorrow don't fit the stereotype of "successful Christian living." But have you considered that Jesus, as a man, experienced every human emotion—even the negative ones? Does that mean that Jesus was not a success? Hardly! Emotions are not intrinsically good or bad—feelings are morally neutral. It is what we do in response to our feelings that characterizes them as bad or good, sinful or righteous. In response to anger, Jesus cleared the Temple in Jerusalem of money changers and livestock—a very righteous act born out of his anger at sin.

Negative and positive emotions are intended by God to be motivational instruments that move us in a positive direction. Whatever emotions we experience are *good* if they move us in the right direction. The emotions themselves are neutral; it is the results that will be positive or negative.

Many Christians tend to deny their negative emotions. Said another way, many Christians are not willing to accept the fact that they have negative feelings. Others try to push their negative emotions onto the back burner and disregard them. It is far more productive to identify and accept our feelings and then to seek constructive ways of responding. Feelings are like thermometers. They report whether we are hot or cold, whether all is well or not so well. If all is well, then we can celebrate. If emotions indicate that all is not well, we can take positive action to correct the situation.

Giving emotional support to your spouse begins by allowing positive and negative emotions. It means celebrating the positive emotions and affirming the negative emotions. To use the biblical phrase, it is "rejoicing with those who rejoice and weeping with those who weep."[6] Because of personality differences, we sometimes find this difficult. I remember the woman who said to me in the counseling office, "I don't understand my husband. Our baby has been sick for the last three months. My mother is battling cancer. The future of his job is uncertain. Yet he comes home excited that he got a fifty-cents-an-hour pay raise."

Because of her personality, her bent toward focusing on the negative, she had a hard time rejoicing with her husband over his small success. Instead, she said to him, "What good is that if you lose your job in three weeks?" He lashed out at her for being so negative and then left the room and remained silent for the rest of the evening. How different things might have been had she been emotionally supportive by saying something like "Honey, that's great. That must mean they like the way you do your job. I'm so proud of you, no matter what happens in the future." By celebrating his small success, she would motivate him to pursue larger successes. By being emotionally supportive, she would be helping her husband succeed.

When your spouse has negative emotions—such as anger, disappointment, depression, or sorrow—you can be emotionally supportive by affirming those emotions and expressing belief in your spouse. Myra came home from the doctor's office and told her husband, Mike, "The doctor said I might lose the baby. We won't know for another week or so, but it's not looking good. I feel so discouraged. I had hoped that this time everything would go well. I don't know what's wrong with me." She was feeling disappointment, frustration, and sadness, and she was focusing the blame on herself.

If Mike wants to be emotionally supportive, he might say, "I can understand why you would feel disappointed. I feel that way too. It's frustrating when we have both tried so hard. When you say, 'I don't know what's wrong with me,' though, it sounds like you are blaming yourself. I guess if I were in your shoes, I might feel the same way, but I want you to know that is not the way I see it. I think you have done everything right. I think if something happens to this baby, we will have to trust God. I just want you to know that I love you, and I will walk with you through this experience. Let's pray together."

Mike is being emotionally supportive of Myra. He is allowing her to have feelings of disappointment and sadness. He is affirming her feelings by saying, "If I were in your shoes, I might feel the same way." But he is being honest about his own perspective, and he is assuring her of his support no matter what. That is the kind of emotional support that often makes the difference between success and failure.

A fourth way to foster success is by expressing respect for your spouse. Because we are made in the image of God, we are creatures of great value: male and female. Something deep within us affirms that we are creatures of respect and dignity, that God's imprint is upon us. Consequently, demeaning words and behavior make us feel violated. When words and actions affirm our inherent worth, we feel respected.

Respect begins with an attitude: "I acknowledge that you are a creature of extreme worth. God has endowed you with certain abilities, insights, and spiritual gifts. Therefore, I respect you as a person. I will not desecrate your worth by making critical remarks about your intellect, your judgment, or your logic. I will seek to understand and grant you the freedom to think different from the way I think and to experience emotions that I may not experience."

An attitude of respect paves the way for you to *show* respect for your mate. Respect does not indicate that you agree on everything, but it does mean that you give your spouse the freedom to be an individual. No two humans are alike in the way they think and feel. Respect says, "That's an interesting way to look at it," not, "That's the dumbest thing I've ever heard." I am often amazed at how inhumanely spouses sometimes treat each other. I remember one man who said to his wife, "I can't believe that you are a college graduate and think so illogically." Such degrading statements create animosity, not respect.

Allowing your spouse to be who God created him or her to be is the first step toward communicating respect. Trying to argue your spouse into compliance with your own views shows disrespect. To show respect is to look for your mate's God-given *giftedness* and to affirm and encourage his or her uniqueness. Respect gives people the freedom to be who they are, to think what they think, and to feel what they feel. A wife does not expect her husband to agree with her all the time, but neither does she expect him to call her ideas *stupid.* A husband knows he is not always right, but he doesn't want to be called a *liar.*

We can express disagreement respectfully. A wife might say to her husband, "Honey, I don't agree with you, but I know there must be good reasons why you see it that way. When you

131

have time, I would like to hear more of your thoughts on that." A husband might say to his wife, "I'm sorry you feel hurt. That was certainly not my intention. Can we talk about it?"

I met Jonathan in Tuscaloosa, Alabama. He came to my seminar alone. At one of the breaks, he said to me, "How can I respect my wife when she doesn't live a respectable lifestyle? Lisa has been unfaithful to me at least twice, and I'm not sure what's going on now. I've lost all respect for her."

Jonathan raises a very significant question. Not everyone lives a life that is worthy of respect, but we can still respect the inherent worth of the person. Though he couldn't respect Lisa's ungodly lifestyle, he could still respect Lisa, not for what she did but for who she is. Regardless of her behavior, she was made in the image of God and thus is extremely valuable. We must acknowledge that God has given his creatures freedom of choice. Even when people make poor choices, it does not diminish their value as human beings.

When Jonathan's wife sinned against him, it brought pain not only to his heart but also to the heart of God for one simple reason: God and Jonathan both love Lisa, and both know that her behavior is detrimental to her and to their relationship with her. However, if Jonathan puts her down by saying, "I can't believe you would do this. You're such a scumbag. I hate you," he is not pushing her toward success but toward failure. Lisa is not a scumbag. She is a creature of God for whom Jesus died. She has great potential for good and needs God's redemptive touch.

How might Jonathan express respect for his wife in the midst of her failure? He could say, "I'm sure you know that your behavior is hurting me deeply. But what really concerns me is that I know your behavior ultimately will hurt you—and I care about you. In my mind, you are a wonderful person with great potential, and I want to help you reach that potential. I know you must make your own decisions. I'm not trying to control your life; I'm just telling you how much I value you and how much I love you."

Jonathan's respect for Lisa's inherent worth as a human being may well bring her to value herself—and ultimately she may return to God and to Jonathan. If that happens, he will have the joy of forgiving her and cooperating with God in seeing her life redeemed. In his marriage, he will have the pleasure of watching the ice and snow of winter recede as the warming winds of spring begin to take hold.

Regardless of what season your marriage is in, when you discover the joy of helping your spouse succeed, you will begin to establish or restore emotional health, respect, support, and encouragement in your marriage. Watching your spouse succeed is one of the great joys of marriage. It is my conviction that marriage is based on the divine principle that two are better than one. In the very beginning, God said, "It is not good for the man to be alone."[7] God's answer to Adam's aloneness was the creation of Eve and the institution of marriage. His intention was that the two would become "one flesh." This does not mean that in marriage we lose our identity as individuals, but it does mean that we choose to give our lives away for the benefit of the other. When this happens, we both succeed. Together, we accomplish more than either one of us could have accomplished alone. The ultimate purpose of marriage is not sex or happiness or even love. The ultimate purpose of marriage is that a husband and wife will help each other accomplish the purpose for which God created them. When this happens, both spouses experience the ultimate joy of cooperating with God to accomplish his purposes.

STRATEGY 6

Maximize Your Differences

In the fall season of marriage, our differences begin to be magnified; in the winter season, they stand as icy walls that divide us. For example, when Gerald's marriage was in the fall season, he was mildly irritated by the way Marcie loaded the dishwasher; but when winter took hold, he became livid every time he opened the dishwasher door and saw the chaos.

In God's plan our differences were never intended to divide us. In fact, God is the author of diversity. No two snowflakes, fingerprints, or leaves on a tree are exactly alike. When God created mankind, he built into our genetic structure the potential for unlimited diversity. When he instituted marriage as a union of two unique individuals, he knew that he was creating unity out of diversity. Not only are we different because we're male and female, we're different in every aspect of life.

Try taking a walk with your spouse and you'll soon discover that you walk at a different pace and with a different gait. Sit down for a rest and you'll notice that the two of you sit differently. Engage in a conversation and you'll discover that your thoughts are extremely diverse. Set out to accomplish a task such as mowing the grass, vacuuming the carpet, or changing a diaper, and you'll find that each of you has a unique approach.

Even our personalities are different. One spouse may be optimistic, whereas the other is pessimistic. One is quiet; the other is talkative. One is logical and methodical; the other is intuitive. One tends to be organized, with everything in its place; the other spends half a lifetime just looking for keys.

After years of arguing about differences, each trying to convince the other that his or her way is the best way, couples often conclude that they are incompatible. In fact, incompatibility—or "irreconcilable differences"—is often given as the grounds for divorce. After thirty years of counseling married couples, I am convinced there are no irreconcilable differences, only people who refuse to reconcile.

In God's mind our differences are designed to be complementary, not to cause conflicts. This principle is illustrated by the Christian church, described in 1 Corinthians 12 as being similar to the human body—composed of ears, eyes, legs, feet, hands, arms, and so forth. Each member of the church is seen as an important part of the body. When everyone works in unity, each part enhances the others and together they serve the purposes of God.

Similarly, in the institution of marriage, God intends for husbands and wives to bring their unique characteristics together to form one team that will work together under God's direction to accomplish his eternal purposes. God designed our differences to be assets, not liabilities. When we learn to maximize our differences for the benefit of the marriage, we align our lives with God's purposes. The Bible calls this marital unity.[1] When each spouse recognizes and affirms the other's uniqueness, the differences themselves weld the couple into an unbeatable team.

So how do we tap into this reality in our marriages? How do we "maximize our differences" in order to move from fall or winter into spring or summer?

IDENTIFY YOUR DIFFERENCES

The process begins with identifying your differences. If you and your spouse are going to maximize your unique qualities, you need to know the ways in which you're different. This is not a difficult task, but it will require some time and thought. The most obvious differences will be those that are the most irritating. Therefore, one way to identify your differences is to make a list of all the things that irritate you about your spouse. After you've made your list, ask yourself two questions:

Why do these things irritate me?

What differences do these irritations reveal?

In most cases, the reason you get irritated is because your spouse doesn't do something the way you would do it. You and your spouse are simply different in these areas, and thus far in your marriage you have seen these differences as irritations. But let's look a little deeper to identify the differences that these irritations reveal. For example, why was Gerald irritated by the way Marcie loaded the dishwasher? Very likely it was because he tends to be organized in his approach to life, whereas Marcie tends to be spontaneous—a common difference observed in many married couples. This difference will show up not only in how they load the dishwasher but in other aspects of life as well.

The following list of common differences between husbands and wives may help you identify some of the differences in your own marriage:

① Talkers often marry people who are quiet and reflective.

② Early risers often marry those who "don't do mornings."

③ People who "like to make things happen" often marry people who enjoy reading about what happens.

④ People who live by the philosophy, "A place for everything and everything in its place" often marry those whose most common question is "Where is it?"

⑤ Planners often marry people who want to work out the details as they go along.

⑥ Homebodies often marry partygoers.

⑦ People who say, "Let's be logical," often marry those who say, "But it doesn't feel right."

⑧ Penny-pinchers often marry spenders, who say, "You can't take it with you."

⑨ Avid readers often marry TV addicts.

⑩ Joggers often marry swimmers.

⑪ Channel surfers often marry commercial watchers.

⑫ And, somehow, country-western devotees marry symphony lovers.

I am sure you can add to this list, but perhaps it will get you started in identifying your differences.[2]

LOOK FOR ASSETS IN YOUR DIFFERENCES

Every difference has a positive side. We don't have to see our differences as irritations. For example, Joe is by nature a couch potato. His wife, Millie, is a butterfly, who is always doing something. She seldom simply sits. In the past, she viewed Joe as lazy; he viewed her as a nervous female who can't relax. They often had words over this difference, but most of the time they simply lived with a low-grade resentment of each other. In my office Joe said, "Why can't she relax and have fun? Life is short; we don't need to work all the time." Millie responded, "But there is so much that needs to be done. I can't believe he can sit there and watch television and leave everything for me to do."

What difference do these irritations reveal? It appears that Joe by nature tends to take a more relaxed and laid-back approach to life, whereas Millie by nature is an activist and tends to be very conscientious. Her theme is "Why sit still when you can be doing something productive?" Joe's theme is "Why work when you can relax?"

Now that this difference has been identified, let's look for the assets. What is the positive side to Joe's approach to life? He reminds me of the old adage, "All work and no play makes Jack a dull boy." He brings to the table the idea that life is to be enjoyed and that there is to be a balance between work and relaxation. Incidentally, the Bible strongly supports this attitude. God himself worked six days and rested on the seventh, and he instructs us to do the same.[3] Scripture also says that life involves a balance between numerous activities. God has "made everything beautiful in its time."[4]

On the other hand, what asset does Millie bring to the equation? Her approach to life reminds us that we each have a solemn responsibility to work. "Life is not a bowl of cherries"; it requires discipline and determination. The Bible supports this idea. The apostle Paul said, "If a man will not work, he shall not eat."[5] Scripture also warns against the dangers of idleness.[6] When we look for the positive side of our differences, we have taken a step in the direction of maximizing our differences.

What about differences that involve immoral behavior? For example, he lies; she doesn't. She finds his lies extremely irritating, and he finds her commitment to truth equally irritating. It

139

is my conviction that there is no asset in immoral behavior. Such behavior calls for repentance and forgiveness, which in turn (and in time) lead to reconciliation. We discussed this process as part of Strategy 1, when we talked about dealing with past failures.

Most of the differences that irritate us in the normal flow of life do not involve immorality. They are simply expressions of our unique design, and there is always a positive side to our uniqueness. If we are to maximize our differences in marriage, we must look for the assets.

LEARN FROM YOUR DIFFERENCES

Remember, God's design for our differences is that they be complementary. They are not intended to divide us but to unite us. Ask God to show you what you need to learn from your differences. Millie needs to learn that life is more than work. For the benefit of her mental and marital health, she may need to take time to sit with Joe and relax while watching a movie. Perhaps she can learn more about the rhythm of work and relaxation. To do so will enrich her life and her marriage. On the other hand, perhaps Joe can learn that as a husband who cares for his wife as Christ cares for the church, he needs to take more initiative to help her do things around the house. If he takes the servant attitude of Christ, he may well ask her, "What could I do to help you this evening?" Doing those things before he sits down to relax may make it easier for her to sit down with him.

There are always lessons to be learned from our differences. None of us has reached the apex of Christian maturity. God's intention is that marriage will stimulate our spiritual, intellectual, and emotional growth. When we look for the lessons in our differences, we will find them and benefit from them.

REPLACE CONDEMNATION WITH AFFIRMATION

A key aspect of learning from our differences is replacing condemnation with affirmation. When we view our differences as irritations, we typically deliver sermons of condemnation to our spouse: "I can't believe you are so lazy" or "Why can't you sit down and relax with me? Why do you always have to be doing something?" Such criticisms perpetuate the winter season of marriage and build icy blocks of resentment.

However, once we understand that our differences are designed to be positive not negative, we can replace condemnation with words of affirmation. Millie might begin by saying, "I know that I have gotten upset with you in the past about how much time you spend in front of the television and how you don't help me with things around the house. But I am beginning to realize that God made us different for a purpose, and I need to learn from you how to relax and enjoy life more and not be so obsessed with getting everything done. So I want to thank you for being the person you are." Such an affirming statement may even solicit a hug from Joe. Whatever his response, he now feels more accepted by her.

Joe might begin by saying, "I know that in the past I've been critical of you for how you're always on the move, never stopping to smell the roses. But I'm beginning to realize that God made us different for a purpose, and I want you to know that I appreciate all your hard work and how you keep things flowing smoothly around here. I know you would like me to help from time to time, and I want to do that more often."

Both partners in a marriage need to feel appreciation rather than condemnation. Mutual affirmation creates an atmosphere for positive change. By now you have no doubt begun to see how the various strategies can work together to move a marriage out

141

of a fall or winter season and into spring or summer. Regardless of where you're starting, there is always a positive first step you can take to begin changing the season of your marriage.

DISCOVER A PLAN FOR MAXIMIZING YOUR DIFFERENCES

Now that you have established a pattern of affirmation and cooperation, you can begin to explore a plan for maximizing your differences. Millie, realizing that she needs to have a more balanced lifestyle, may offer to spend thirty minutes each evening on the couch with Joe, talking or watching TV with him—simply seeking to relax and unwind from the cares of the day. Joe may say to Millie, "I know that I need to help you more around the house. In the past, I have resented the fact that you were always doing something and never had time for me. I really wanted to help you; I just didn't want to spend the whole evening working. But because I do want to have the attitude of Christ, why don't we identify some things I could do that would help you the most, so we can both have time to relax together?" With this attitude, Joe and Millie will learn how to maximize their differences. When they do, not only will they be a compatible team, but they will more effectively accomplish the purposes that God has for each of their lives.

Now let's go back to Gerald, who loaded the dishwasher like an engineer, and Marcie, who loaded it as if she were playing Frisbee. His personality is strong on organization, whereas hers is strong on spontaneity. How might they maximize their differences? Perhaps they could agree that Gerald would be the team member who would load the dishwasher, because his method tends to produce cleaner dishes and fewer broken glasses. On those evenings when he has a meeting and Marcie loads the dishwasher, he would allow her the freedom to do it her way. He knows that when he unloads the dishwasher the next morning, he might find spoons still covered with peanut butter and maybe a chipped glass or two; but he realizes that these issues aren't the end of the world. The dirty spoons can soak in the measuring cup that she forgot to put in the dishwasher, and the glasses can be replaced. After all, he's married to a spontaneous woman who keeps his life exciting. It's a small price to pay for such a treasure. Maximizing our skills and minimizing our weaknesses are part of moving us back to the springtime of marriage.

FIVE STEPS TO MAXIMIZE YOUR DIFFERENCES

1. Identify your differences.

2. Look for assets in your differences.

3. Learn from your differences.

4. Replace condemnation with affirmation.

5. Discover a plan for maximizing your differences.

143

What if your spouse is not willing to work with you on maximizing your differences? What if he or she is locked into one way of doing things and is not even willing to discuss your differences? All is not lost. You still have the power of influence. In the next chapter, I want to help you learn how to use your influence in a positive way. Even if your spouse initially won't participate or cooperate, you can still create positive changes in your marriage.

STRATEGY 7

Implement the Power of Positive Influence

If your marriage is in the season of winter or fall, you are probably reading this book alone. You wish that your spouse would read it. You wish he or she would be willing to implement the strategies that would move your marriage forward to the spring and summer seasons. But based on past experience and your current circumstances, you have little hope that he or she will do so.

Todd, who has been married for fourteen years, expressed his frustration: "I feel trapped in so many instances. It doesn't matter what I say—it always leads to issues. I am very concerned about giving up on my marriage, because I have so much invested. My wife has gone to work in the last year, which helps; but she brings her work home, and I feel like I have no say in things, yet she tries to manage all the details of my life. I guess you can read the frustration in my writing. I harbor bitterness toward her. We are not dealing with the issues, and I'm tired of listening to the same whining over and over. I want to have a better marriage, but I'm not sure it's going to happen. I am deeply concerned. That is why I came to this seminar even though she would not come with me."

Sonya expressed a similar sense of hopelessness. She is in her third marriage and has been married for three-and-a-half years. "At present, our marriage is in the fall season. It is producing high anxiety. The presence of anger is stagnating our relationship. Conflicts over the children bring great sadness. At times it is overwhelming and causes a spirit of defeat. Constant struggles are creating a future of uncertainty for us and the children. All these rampant emotions bring fear. I am very concerned about our relationship. I have asked my husband to go for counseling, but he refuses. I don't know what else to do."

Strategy 7 is for people like Sonya and Todd, who are willing to work on their marriages but find little encouragement from their spouses. Although these husbands and wives sincerely hope that things will get better, many of them believe they have already done all they can to deal with the issues that have kept them from marital unity. Most are discouraged with the results. If they have gone for counseling, it has not been productive. If they have read books, they have read them alone, wishing their spouse would hear what the author is saying and be moved to change. Some have tried the method of gentle confrontation but have been met with a silent audience and no response. Some, in desperation, have tried yelling and screaming. Their pain has been so intense that they have actually lost control trying to express it. Their loud cries for help have brought a counterattack or withdrawal. Consequently, some husbands and wives have resigned themselves to the idea that their spouse will never change and they are left with only two options—tolerate a life of misery or get out of the marriage and hope for something better. Once they choose between these two sorry alternatives, they become prisoners of their decision. Thousands of people live in these self-made prisons because they fail to understand the power of positive influence.

It is true that you cannot change your spouse, but it is equally true that you can and do influence your spouse every day. Because we are individuals and because we have free will, no one can force us to change our thoughts or behavior. On the other hand, because we are also relational creatures, we are influenced by everyone with whom we interact. We're influenced by what we hear and see. Advertisers make millions of dollars each year because of this reality. They do not *make* us buy their products, but they do influence us. Otherwise, they would stop advertising.

The power of influence has profound implications for the seasons of marriage. However, we must first acknowledge that we cannot directly change our spouses' personality or behavior. We cannot control how they think or feel or the words that come out of their mouths. We can make requests, but we cannot be assured that they will respond positively to our requests.

If we mistakenly believe that we can directly change our spouses' behavior, we will likely spend our time trying to manipulate them. The idea behind manipulation is that if I do *this,* my spouse will be forced to do *that.* If I can make him happy enough, he will respond to my request; or, if I can make her miserable enough, she will respond to my request. However, every effort at manipulation will ultimately fail for one simple reason: Our spouses have the freedom to choose their response. The moment they realize that we are trying to control them by manipulation, they rebel. No one wants to be manipulated or controlled.

Even though you cannot directly control your spouse's attitudes and actions, you do have the ability to influence him or her—either positively or negatively, by word or by deed. Every time you encounter your spouse, you exert a subtle influence. If

147

your spouse walks into the room, gives you a hug and a kiss, and says, "I love you; I've missed you today," he or she has influenced you in a positive way. However, if your spouse walks into the house, fails to acknowledge your presence, and goes straight to the computer room or the refrigerator, or if your spouse walks in and immediately criticizes your appearance or behavior, he or she has influenced you in a negative way. Everything you do or say (or don't do or say) influences your spouse—for better or for worse. Your words and behavior can either cause your spouse tremendous pain, hurt, and discouragement (like the icy winds of winter) or be a soothing balm that powerfully influences your spouse in the direction of positive change (like the warm breezes of summer).

Over the years I have tested this strategy with numerous individuals in troubled marriages. When a husband or wife is willing to choose a positive attitude that leads to positive actions, the change in the spouse is often radical. One woman said, "I can't believe what has happened to my husband. I never dreamed he could be as loving and kind as he has been for the last three months. This is more change than I ever anticipated." The power of positive influence holds tremendous potential for troubled marriages. When all is said and done, you will have had a positive or a negative impact on your spouse. Which will it be? The choice is yours.

CHOOSING TO HAVE A POSITIVE IMPACT

If I got out of bed only on the mornings when I really felt like getting out of bed, I would be covered with bedsores. I go against my *feelings* almost every morning and *choose* to get up because I desire to do something positive with my life. Normally, before the day is over, I feel good about having gotten up. My positive choices lead to positive actions that result in positive feelings. I feel good about myself because I have invested my day wisely.

POSITIVE CHOICES lead to POSITIVE ACTIONS that result in POSITIVE FEELINGS

The same principle applies to marriage. When I *choose* to have a positive influence on my wife, regardless of how I might *feel,* my positive choices lead to positive actions that result in positive feelings—for both me *and* my wife. Choosing to implement the power of positive influence is good for your own mental health, in addition to the positive impact it will have on your spouse.

Where do we begin? Perhaps you can identify with the woman who said to me, "Our marriage has been so dysfunctional for so long, I don't know where to start." The first step in any positive change is to recognize and acknowledge that you have a choice. You don't have to be controlled by your emotions—or your spouse's emotions. You don't have to respond in the same old way to the same old provocations. You can choose a different response. Even if the biggest obstacle in your marriage is your own past behavior and attitudes, you don't have to stay stuck there. Just because you've "made your bed" doesn't mean you have to lie in it. You can choose to get up and make a positive investment in your marriage.

You may feel hurt, disappointed, frustrated, or even angry in your marriage, but these emotions need not control your behavior. Emotions are to be acknowledged and processed, but they are not to be the controlling factor in our lives. If we allow angry feelings to control our behavior, we may lash out with critical, condemning words or physical abuse. On the other hand, we may say to ourselves, "I feel angry. I feel hurt, disappointed, and frustrated. But I want to have a positive influence on my spouse, and I refuse to be controlled by these emotions." Positive change begins with positive choices.

Once you have decided to implement the power of positive influence in your marriage, you are ready to begin utilizing the six other strategies discussed in this book. After thirty years of counseling married couples, I know of no better approach.

Let's assume for a moment the worst-case scenario: Your spouse is unwilling to read this book, is unwilling to go for counseling, is unwilling to even talk about your marriage, and appears to be totally closed to the idea of improving your marriage. Perhaps he or she is even critical of your efforts. If this is true, you may be feeling all the emotions of winter and fall. I am not encouraging you to deny these feelings. Rather, I am encouraging you to admit your feelings but not be controlled by them.

The decision to implement the power of positive influence may be the most significant decision you have ever made in your marriage. Therefore, I am inviting you to join me in walking through the first six strategies again, looking at them from the perspective of someone in your situation. At the moment, your spouse may not be willing to join you in the journey, but I want you to acknowledge that he or she cannot keep you from making the journey. As we travel, I will introduce you to individuals who have tried these strategies and reaped the benefits.

STRATEGY 1: DEAL WITH PAST FAILURES

Anna had been married eight years when her marriage quickly turned to winter. "I guess we had been in the fall season for some time," she said. "It's just that I didn't recognize it. One day I overheard my husband say to someone on the phone, 'I'll miss you, too.' I knew this was not a business conversation. In my heart, I knew he was talking to another woman. I didn't want to believe it, so I didn't say anything about it. But when the phone bill came, I checked the numbers and found numerous calls to a number I didn't recognize.

"Then one night, the phone rang. I answered it and a lady asked to speak with Rob. I told her that he was not home at the moment and asked if she would like for him to call her back. She said yes and gave me her number. Immediately, I matched the number and knew that this was the lady Rob had been calling. When I confronted him, he admitted that the call was from a woman at work but assured me that there was no sexual relationship—it was 'just a friendship.' But I knew there was more to it. I was so hurt and angry. I couldn't believe that he had betrayed me. I withdrew in silence. I didn't talk to Rob for two weeks. Then I told him I wanted out of the marriage, that I couldn't live with a man I couldn't trust. He said, 'You are making more of this than it is. I have not been unfaithful to you. I told you it was just a friendship.' I said, 'You don't call someone sixteen times in two weeks and call it a friendship. And I don't know how many times you called her on your cell phone.' I was furious!

"The next day I saw a counselor. I didn't want to leave Rob without talking with someone. I knew that I was so angry I was likely to do something I would later realize was foolish. I went to the counselor twice a week for the next three weeks. In the early sessions, she listened to my rage and helped me take a realistic look at my marriage. She pointed out that this situation did not happen overnight. I began to realize that part of this was my fault. I had been so involved with our two preschool children that I had basically ignored Rob's needs. I had been very critical of him for not helping me the way I thought he should. I asked myself the question, 'If I were a man, would I want to come home to a woman like me?' My answer devastated me. I knew I had failed

Rob. Now, that did not excuse his behavior, but I knew I had to deal with my own failure first.

"At first I resisted the idea. I said, 'But why should I confess my failures when he is the one involved with someone else?' The counselor did not excuse Rob's behavior, but she affirmed that if I wanted to find healing for my marriage, I needed to deal with my own failure. It was one of the hardest things I have ever done. I asked God to show me where I had failed Rob over the past eight years. God answered that prayer. I wrote everything down as it came to mind, and I wept. I asked God to forgive me and I prayed for the courage to admit my failures to Rob. Later, my counselor helped me write out a confession statement, which included a list of the things God had brought to my mind.

"One night I said to Rob, 'I know that I have been angry with you for the past few weeks. I've been cold and harsh. I guess that's because I have been hurt so deeply. But as you know, I've been going for counseling, and I have realized that you are not the only one who has sinned in our relationship. The other night, I asked God to show me where I have failed you. And if you are willing to listen, I would like to share what he told me. I have asked him to forgive me, and I would like to ask you to forgive me as well.'

"When I read my list of failures, Rob responded, 'You're beating up on yourself, Anna. You're trying to take responsibility for my failures. There's no excuse for what I've done.'

"I said, 'Rob, I appreciate your saying that. But the fact is, all these things are still true. I have not been the wife you've deserved. With God's help and your willingness, it is going to be different in the future.'

"We continued to talk and eventually Rob said, 'I'm willing to forgive you if you will forgive me. I want to join you in counseling, because I know we can make our marriage better.' That was the night things changed for us. We've been in counseling now for six months. We've made great progress. Our lives are very different. We're learning how to meet each other's needs, and I am so encouraged. I would even say that we are getting near the springtime. And I expect to see the crocuses soon. It's like you said: I could not change Rob, but I could have a positive influence on him by dealing with my own failures. I'm so grateful for the guidance of my counselor, who helped me process my emotions and steered me in the right direction."

I do not wish to imply that in every situation the spouse will reciprocate to the power of positive influence as quickly as Rob did. But I do believe that dealing honestly with your own past failures is the first step in having a positive influence on your spouse. You may take the step of confession and repentance for your failures and your spouse may respond to you harshly. One husband said, "I tried what you suggested and my wife said, 'If you think that a lousy confession is going to change my mind, you are wrong. You have hurt me too deeply. Saying "I'm sorry" is not enough.'" You cannot control your spouse's response, but by confessing your own failures, you will have a positive influence on your spouse whether or not it is evident.

153

The best choice you can make is to deal with your own past failures and leave the results to God. No matter how your spouse responds to your confession, you will have a positive influence because you have followed the instructions of Jesus to "first take the plank out of your own eye."[1]

STRATEGY 2: CHOOSE A WINNING ATTITUDE

If it is the middle of winter in your marriage, a positive attitude can make all the difference. Viktor Frankl, a Jewish doctor imprisoned by the Nazis during World War II, discovered the power of a positive attitude in the midst of a concentration camp:

> *We who lived in the concentration camps can remember the men who walked through the huts comforting others, giving away their last piece of bread. They may have been few in number, but they offer sufficient proof that everything can be taken from a man but one thing: the last of his freedoms—to choose one's attitude in any given set of circumstances, to choose one's own way.*[2]

The men who chose to give away their last pieces of bread were not motivated by their emotions but by their attitudes. Their positive actions affected the emotions and attitudes of their fellow prisoners.

There are some who would object to the idea of having a positive attitude when one is feeling hurt, anger, disappointment, and frustration. They object on the grounds that to think positive when one feels negative is hypocritical. But I believe that is a false premise, and to the degree that it has permeated Western thinking, it has been detrimental to marital relationships. In other areas of life, we often go against our emotions. We may feel discouraged or depressed when a friend calls to invite us to lunch, but we choose to go, put on a smile, and think positive. By the time the lunch is over, our feelings of discouragement may well have lifted, if only momentarily. Our attitudes and actions affect our emotions.

Following the steps suggested in this strategy, you can *choose* a winning attitude. Acknowledge that your negative thinking is making things worse rather than better. Identify your spouse's positive characteristics and choose to thank God for these traits.

Thank God that your spouse is made in his image and is therefore extremely valuable. Thank God that your spouse is uniquely gifted and has a unique role to play in the Kingdom of God. Thank God that marriage was his idea and ask him to give you the ability to be his messenger by communicating positive statements to your spouse. Then begin to express appreciation for the positive traits you observe in your spouse.

You can choose a winning attitude even when your spouse shows no interest in improving your marriage. I first met Stuart in Rome, Georgia. He had been married for fifteen years, and he admitted that he and his wife, Karen, had spent most of those years in the winter season of marriage. "For years, I blamed Karen for our poor marriage. She wanted to be a stay-at-home mom. I agreed to that and worked hard to support the family. The problem, as I saw it, was that she was not doing her part. The house always looked a wreck, and I was lucky if she cooked one meal a week. She was never interested in sex, and frankly, I got to the place where I was not that interested either. We were raising the kids, but our marriage was empty.

"One day, I was reading my Bible in desperation. I stumbled across Philippians 4:8: 'Whatever is true, whatever is noble, whatever is right, whatever is pure, whatever is lovely, whatever is admirable—if anything is excellent or praiseworthy—think about such things.' It was like God said to me, 'You have had a negative attitude about your marriage, and it is not helping. Why don't you begin to focus on the positive? Look for the good things in your wife and begin to give her compliments.'

"I asked God to help me make a list of positive things about Karen. I was amazed at how long the list was. Then I asked him to give me the ability to give her one compliment each day and refrain from making negative statements to her. What happened in the next month was unbelievable. When I stopped criticizing her and began expressing appreciation for the positive things I observed in her, my wife's behavior began to change. She began to smile again and to become flirty like she was when we dated. I'll never forget the first time she initiated sex. I was totally blown away.

"A couple of months later, we had a marriage seminar at our church, and I asked her if she would like to attend. She agreed, and that was another big step forward. We definitely moved from winter to springtime. It was like a whole new relationship. We began talking about our marriage and working through the things that had been painful to both of us in the past. We have made tremendous progress, and I am excited about our future together. I wish everyone could have the kind of marriage we have."

Stuart and Karen's journey from winter to spring began with Stuart's choice to have a winning attitude and his commitment to learn to focus on the positive things about Karen. Often, marital seasons begin to change when one person chooses a winning attitude in spite of negative feelings.

STRATEGY 3: LEARN TO SPEAK YOUR SPOUSE'S LOVE LANGUAGE

Ruth showed up at my office without an appointment. I happened to be free and agreed to see her. She wasted no time in getting to the point. "I have an appointment with an attorney at two o'clock," she said. "I'm going to divorce my husband. Twenty years of misery is long enough. I don't know why I came by your office. I don't think there is anything you can do, but I guess I thought I should at least talk to a counselor before I see the attorney."

I listened for the next hour as Ruth poured out her story of pain. It was basically a story of neglect. Her husband was an auto mechanic, who had his garage in the backyard of their home. He was a hardworking man but apparently knew little about relating to his wife. From her perspective, "He expects me to have his meals prepared, wash and iron his clothes, and have sex when he desires. Other than that, he has no time for me. And if I happen to be late in preparing one of the meals, he curses me out. He spends his evenings working in the shop, except on Wednesday nights when he goes out with the boys to drink. Usually, he doesn't get drunk, and when he does, he is not abusive. He mainly sleeps on the couch that night. I just feel that I cannot continue in this relationship," she said.

I was deeply sympathetic with Ruth, but I took the opportunity to explain to her the power of unconditional love. I shared with her the concept of the five love languages, and I told her about the love tank. When I suggested that her husband's love tank had probably been empty all his life, except for the brief time when he and Ruth were "in love," she responded, "It's interesting that you would say that. When we were dating, he was kind to me. I really thought I was marrying a good man, but after the wedding everything changed." I suggested that when her husband came down off the emotional high of their dating relationship, he reverted to his normal emotional state, which was one of an empty love tank.

I challenged Ruth to a six-months-long experiment. I asked her to speak her husband's primary love language once a week to see what might happen. She was not overly enthusiastic about the project, but she agreed. She called the attorney and put the divorce on hold. What happened over the next three months was, in her words, "Unbelievable. If anyone had told me that my husband would start speaking my love language and that I would have love feelings for him again, I would have said it was impossible. The fact is, I do have love feelings for him, and he is speaking my love language. I wish I had known the power of love twenty years ago. I can't believe I waited so long to get help."

Not all spouses will respond to expressions of love as quickly as Ruth's husband did, but most husbands and wives are desperately in need of emotional love. When they receive it unconditionally, they begin to experience positive feelings toward their spouses. Eventually, many will reciprocate those expressions of love, moving the marriage out of fall or winter and into the seasons of spring and summer. Your decision to love in spite of your hurt may be the most significant decision you ever make.

STRATEGY 4: DEVELOP THE AWESOME POWER OF EMPATHETIC LISTENING

I was leading a series of marriage enrichment classes at a local church when I met Marc. One of our sessions focused on empathetic listening. Marc stayed after class and told me the frustration he was experiencing in his marriage: "My wife, Carol, is hypercritical of everything I do. I feel no support from her. I try to work hard, but it is very discouraging when she puts down everything I do. She criticizes the way I relate to the children. She is critical of my relationship with my mother. Actually, I see my mom very little now because I don't want to hear Carol's angry words about her. She says I don't listen to her, and maybe I don't. But how can I listen when everything I hear is critical?"

I agreed to spend some individual time with Marc to see if we could come up with a strategy that might stimulate growth in his marriage. He assured me that his wife would not come for counseling. He had suggested it before, but she was not open to it. Over the next several weeks, I shared with Marc that most hypercritical people speak out of hurt, anger, and an empty love tank. I tried to help him understand that the road to healing often begins with an empathetic listener. I assured him that I knew it would not be easy, but if he wanted to have a positive influence on his wife, empathetic listening was probably the best way to start. I explained that the goal was to see the world through the eyes of his spouse and thus understand what she was experiencing. We talked about how to listen without judging and how to affirm his wife even when he disagreed with her ideas. It took a while, but I knew that Marc was beginning to get the idea of the power of empathetic listening. We worked on some of the listening skills discussed in Strategy 4, and Marc began the hard work of really listening to his wife.

159

What happened over the next few months was more than either of us had anticipated. When Marc re-engaged in his marriage, using empathetic listening as his main strategy, his wife's critical attitude began to soften. It was probably two months before he noticed any difference, and even then it was only that she was calmer in her expressions of displeasure. "But I guess she realized that I was listening to her," Marc said, "so she didn't need to scream at me. I think the biggest thing that happened was that I began to understand her better. I had no idea that she carried so much hurt inside. I realized that I had not caused all her pain, but I had added to it by not understanding what was going on inside her."

Within six months, Carol was willing to start individual counseling to deal with some of her past hurts. Later, she and Marc spent six months in marital counseling together. Today, they have a healthy marriage; in fact, they lead marriage-enrichment classes at their church. Never underestimate the power of empathetic listening.

STRATEGY 5: DISCOVER THE JOY OF HELPING YOUR SPOUSE SUCCEED

Barbara was in my office complaining about her husband, Richard. "He wants to be a real estate salesman. For the past six months, he's spent every spare minute studying for the real estate exam. I don't think he has the personality to be a salesman. He says I'm not supportive of him, but I'm just trying to help him be realistic."

"Has he tried selling real estate before?" I asked.

"No," she said, "but he tried selling cars, and that didn't go very well. He thinks he's found his niche, but he has been working for a real estate company for six weeks now and hasn't sold a house. We can't pay the bills on my salary, and who knows when he is going to get a check?"

I could tell that Barbara was extremely frustrated. All her conversations with Richard had not seemed to quell his desire to sell real estate. It took three or four counseling sessions before Barbara was able to accept the idea that because Richard had spent so much time in preparation to pass the Realtor's exam and because he had persisted in spite of her efforts to dissuade him, maybe he could succeed in the real estate business.

In time, Barbara came to understand that his success or failure might depend on her emotional support. "How far in debt would you be if Richard did not bring home a check for one year?" I asked. The next week, Barbara came back with a figure. I suggested that she and Richard borrow that amount of money and draw on it as needed, while together seeking to make him a successful real estate salesman. "If he succeeds," I reasoned, "the loan can be easily repaid. If he fails, it is not an exorbitant amount for the two of you to pay while he works at another job. At least you will know whether real estate is Richard's niche."

With this emotional security, Barbara bought the idea of helping Richard become a success. She was going against her fears, but she knew that he deserved to have her support in a project to which he had devoted so much time and energy. I warned her against trying to take over his business and telling him how to be successful. Rather, her role was to be supportive by expressing interest in his daily experiences and rejoicing in any small victory that came. If he became disappointed from losing a sale, her response would be "I'm sure I would feel disappointed if I were in your shoes as well. But that's part of sales. We'll just look for the next one and believe the best. You want to be a success at this, and I know you can do it."

At the end of the year, the loan had been repaid and Richard and Barbara had a small savings account. The second year was even better. Over the past ten years, there have certainly been ups and downs, but Richard has become one of his company's best salesmen. He and Barbara can laugh now about their one-year experiment. But Richard knows that without her support, he probably would not have made it. Barbara takes great joy in knowing that she helped her husband succeed at something he really wanted to do.

As a by-product of his business, Richard learned some principles at various sales seminars that would also enhance his marriage. He learned how to communicate with Barbara in a positive way and how to encourage her with affirming words. Together, they have been smelling the roses of summer for several years.

Of course, Richard might also have failed in the real estate business. But with Barbara's support, he probably would have recognized it sooner and turned from it with dignity rather than defeat. Helping your spouse succeed may involve walking together through some failures, but at least you will be walking *together*. Remember, keeping your marriage in the spring and summer seasons does not necessarily mean there won't be some poison ivy and yellow jackets along the way, but a unified marriage will be better able to weather the adversity and stay strong.

What desires has your spouse expressed? In what ways might you be supportive of these desires? Helping your spouse succeed is a positive strategy for improving your marriage.

STRATEGY 6: MAXIMIZE YOUR DIFFERENCES

Brad was a morning person. Before marriage, he had dreams of having breakfast with his wife, discussing the prospects of the day, and praying together before work. After marriage, he discovered that Jenny "didn't do mornings." While he jumped out of bed like a jack-in-the-box, she eased into the morning like a bear waking up from hibernation. For the first several years of their marriage, Brad resented Jenny. He usually held his frustration inside, but occasionally he would accuse her of being lazy. He would tell her that she should go to bed earlier or that all she needed was a good cup of coffee.

There were other differences that also frustrated Brad. He liked to hike, but Jenny was not a hiker. When they dated, she had accompanied him on a couple of treks, but she couldn't figure why anyone would want to walk through the woods and run the risk of picking up ticks or being bitten by a snake. She'd been raised in the city and thought that the woods were for animals, not humans. She liked to go to symphonies. Brad preferred rock concerts.

Within a few years, Brad was convinced he had made a serious mistake in marrying Jenny. "The differences were too great. I didn't see any way that we would ever get it together," he said. "Then one day, I read a book on marriage. I guess I was pretty desperate, and I thought maybe I would find something that could help me. In a chapter titled 'Differences: The Grounds for Compatibility,' the author talked about the fact that all couples have differences. Some learn to work together as a team and others simply spend a lifetime arguing."

He knew that Jenny would not read the book, but he knew that he had a strategy for improving their marriage. "So I made a list of all the things that irritated me about Jenny and began to ask myself, 'What are the positive aspects of our differences?' It was amazing what I began to see. I realized that Jenny's propensity to sleep in provided me a wonderful setting for my personal quiet time with God. I could have an uninterrupted time with God before I began my day. I realized what a blessing that was. So I thanked God for making us different. When Jenny tried to hike with me, I was always on her case because she never kept up. This irritated me and made the hike less enjoyable for her. For me, hiking was a way of unwinding from the pressures of life—relaxing in the beauty of nature and realizing that life was not a rat race. I enjoyed hiking alone much more than the frustration of hiking with Jenny. So I thanked God for giving me a wife who encouraged me to hike alone. I learned that in all our differences, there was a positive side that I had failed to see.

"After I started thanking God for the differences, I found myself appreciating Jenny more, and eventually I got around to telling her how much I appreciated her. My former words of condemnation became words of commendation. In time—it didn't happen overnight—Jenny's attitude toward me changed. When I allowed her to be the person God had made her to be and recognized the positive things about her personality, she began to affirm me and the emotional warmth came back into our marriage. I hate to think what would have happened to us if I had not discovered the truth that differences are the grounds for a compatible marriage."

Your spouse may be unwilling to read this book with you or to work with you on a strategy for maximizing your differences. But you can begin the process by recognizing your spouse's positive traits, thanking God for them, and expressing your appreciation. When you take the initiative and seek to maximize your differences, you are implementing the power of positive influence. This power may well lead your marriage out of the dead of winter and into a more enjoyable season. As one woman said to me, "After all that had happened in our marriage, if someone had told me that I would have loving feelings for my husband again, I would have said, 'No way!' But I do. He has asked me for forgiveness and is really trying to work on our marriage. I never thought that day would come. It makes all my efforts worthwhile. Given time, I think we will see spring and summer again." Through perseverance, prayer, and positive action, she was reaping the fruit of implementing the power of positive influence.

PART III

Putting Your Plan into Practice

MOVING FORWARD
FROM HERE AND NOW

Now that you've had an initial exposure to the four seasons of marriage and seven strategies for enhancing the seasons of your marriage, I want to challenge you and encourage you to develop a plan for applying these principles to your marriage. I wrote this book to give you a simple paradigm for understanding the quality of your marriage and to give you some practical steps that will enable you to develop the kind of marriage that God designed for you.

God did not create marriage to make us miserable. According to his design, a husband will love his wife as Christ loved the church; he will give his life away in ministry and service to his wife. In this climate of love, according to God's design, a wife will be free to reciprocate her husband's love and to find ways to invest her life in service to him. When a husband and wife both live according to God's design for them, they will be mutually submitted to each other and looking out for each other's best interest. In this free and loving partnership, they will be able to accomplish the purpose that God has for their life together.

God designed just such a marriage for you. The reason I feel so strongly about the message of this book is because I have seen these strategies turn literally thousands of marriages from the coldness of winter to the excitement of spring. I *know* they will work for you. But first you must put your plan into practice. Abstract knowledge is of little value, but *applied* knowledge is wisdom.

I will be the first to admit that my marriage to Karolyn is still in process—yes, even after forty-two years. The reality is that *every* marriage is still in process; no one has the perfect marriage. The good news is that you can have a better marriage than you do now. The strategies we have discussed will move your marriage in the right direction.

STRATEGY 1 challenges you to *deal with past failures*. Failure alone will not destroy a marriage, but *unconfessed* and *unforgiven* failure will.

STRATEGY 2 reminds you that *attitude* often makes the difference between winter, spring, summer, or fall. A negative, critical attitude pushes you toward the coldness of winter; whereas a positive attitude, which looks for the best in your spouse and affirms it, leads to the warmth of spring and summer.

STRATEGY 3 encourages you to *discover and speak your spouse's primary love language*. Everyone has a deep emotional need to feel loved. When you meet that need for your spouse, you create a climate in which the crocuses can begin to bloom in your marriage.

STRATEGY 4 gives you the tools to *develop the art of empathetic listening*. When your spouse is talking, the most powerful thing you can do is listen. Only as you listen empathetically will you come to understand your spouse's thoughts, feelings, and desires. Understanding leads to a blossoming of intimacy.

STRATEGY 5 helps you *discover the joy of helping your spouse succeed.* Few accomplishments in life are more satisfying or have greater results than helping your spouse accomplish the purposes for which God designed him or her. Implement this strategy and share the rewards of true success.

STRATEGY 6 teaches you how to *maximize your differences.* God made husbands and wives different for a purpose—a *positive* purpose. When you learn how to turn your differences into assets, you and your spouse will both be winners.

STRATEGY 7 shows you how to *implement the power of positive influence.* Your spouse may not be willing to read this book or discuss strategies for improving your marriage, but that doesn't mean your efforts will be in vain. Although you cannot control your spouse's behavior, you can choose to exert a positive influence. Perhaps the most powerful way to influence your spouse is by applying the concepts you've learned in Strategies 1–6.

Take the first step: Ask your spouse to read Part I, which describes the four seasons. Then take the Marital Seasons Profile, which will help you identify the season of your marriage. Discuss the results with each other and express your desire for growth and improvement. I hope that you and your spouse will read this book together, discuss the seven strategies, and seek to implement them. If you do, I'm confident you will find that the seasons of your marriage will be greatly enriched and enhanced.

FOUR SEASONS Q&A

QUESTION

I really want a better marriage, but I don't have much hope. I have read Strategy 7 on the power of influence, but nothing I do seems to make any difference. When I've tried in the past, my spouse has been unwilling to make any changes. I don't know if it's worth the effort to try again.

ANSWER

I am deeply sympathetic with your lack of hope. When your best efforts are met with resistance or apathy, it's easy to get discouraged. However, the fact that you have seen little or no change in the past does not mean that your spouse is incapable of making changes in the future. Your attitudes and behavior constantly influence your spouse—for better or for worse. Although it may seem as if you are having little influence on your spouse's behavior, your influence is actually quite profound. The strategies I have shared in this book, when applied consistently, have helped thousands of couples effectively stimulate marital growth. Don't allow the apparent failure of past efforts to keep you from trying these strategies in your marriage.

Some people are more successful at completing projects when they are working with a group, or at least with one other person. For example, many people who have unsuccessfully tried to lose weight on their own have finally succeeded when they joined a weight-loss program that involves a regular meeting with other people. If this has been your experience, then perhaps you could share this book with a friend who is in a marital season similar to yours. The two of you could meet regularly to discuss the seven strategies and your efforts to implement them. The first step—the decision to try again—is often the hardest. But trying holds the potential for positive change. The farmer who never plants the seed will not reap a harvest.

QUESTION

What if I try a strategic action that I believe is positive but it rubs my spouse the wrong way or is perceived as manipulative?

ANSWER

Perhaps the best approach is to be proactive. Before beginning a new strategy, ask your spouse if such behavior on your part will enhance his or her life. For example, let's say you want to initiate Strategy 1: Deal with Past Failures. You might say to your spouse, "I've been thinking about my life, and I know that I am not a perfect spouse. I realize that I have failed you in some rather significant ways. I would like to identify these failures and put them behind me. I really want to be the spouse you deserve. Would you be willing to help me identify my failures and perhaps make some suggestions on what I could do to make life easier for you?"
Your spouse might respond flippantly by saying such things as "Sounds like you've been to church again," or "I thought you'd

*never ask!" Then again, he or she might respond sincerely by say-ing, "I'd be willing to do anything to make our marriage better."
Your spouse's response is not the most important issue. What mat-ters is your honest communication that you are giving serious con-sideration to your marriage, that you have chosen to deal with
past failures, and that you are seeking to take steps of growth.
Informing your spouse of what you are doing may allay his or her
fears and stimulate a positive response when you begin to imple-ment the plan.*

*On the other hand, if you seek to take a positive step in your
marriage and your spouse responds by saying, "I don't like that. I
find it offensive. I feel as if you are trying to manipulate me," it's
time to practice the skills of empathetic listening. You might ask,
"In what way do you see this as being manipulative?" Listen care-fully and ask other clarifying questions. You might say, "Are you
saying that when I do _____, you feel as if I am trying to force you
to do something you don't want to do?" Often, honest dialogue
can help you work through your spouse's initial resistance, lead
you toward implementing positive changes, and make it easier for
your spouse to respond positively. It is certainly possible that what
one person perceives to be a loving action may be interpreted by
the other as an effort to manipulate. That is why Strategy 3 is so
important. Learning to speak your spouse's love language is one of
the keys to moving a marriage toward spring and summer.*

173

❦

QUESTION

If trust has been compromised or destroyed, how do my spouse and I get started on the road to reconciliation?

ANSWER

Most couples enter marriage with a high level of trust in each other. Without trust, they probably would not make the decision to marry. Trust flourishes until one (or both) of the spouses violates the trust—either by lying or by some other act of unfaithfulness. Once trust has been damaged or destroyed, it is not automatically restored when the offending spouse admits, "I was wrong. I'm sorry. Will you forgive me?" Even genuine confession, repentance, and forgiveness do not instantly restore trust.

174

I often describe trust as a fragile plant. Violating trust is like stepping on the plant and pushing it into the mud. Although it has the capacity to straighten up and grow healthy again, it will take time. When trust is violated a second time, it's like breaking off the plant at ground level. The root system is still there, but the trunk of the plant is now gone. It will take even longer for the roots to produce trust again. The only road to restoration is for the offending individual to become trustworthy again. If you're the one who has broken trust, you must consistently do what you say you're going to do and go where you say you are going. In short, you must live a life above reproach. When this happens, trust slowly grows to become healthy again.

If you want your spouse to trust you again, live your life aboveboard. Let your life be an open book. Invite your spouse to "check up on you." Welcome his or her inquiries. Live in such a way that you have nothing to hide. When this happens, you will find that in time your spouse will genuinely trust you again.

ॐ

QUESTION

There's a saying, "Better the devil we know than the devil we don't know." How can couples overcome their fear of negative consequences, which may paralyze them and keep them from pursuing positive change?

ANSWER

Let's face it. Change can be scary. It may take us out of our comfort zone. However, change is inevitable. We cannot avoid it. Change also involves a certain amount of risk, but risk, too, is part of life. We take certain risks when we get into a car and drive onto the highway. Most of us are willing to take the risk because the alternative does not hold the potential that we desire.

The same is true when we seek to initiate change in a marital relationship. There is always the risk that the process may provoke arguments. We may verbalize thoughts and feelings that have been dormant for months or perhaps years. We may hear things that cause us pain. On the other hand, if we don't initiate change, we will hamper our potential for positive movement. Therefore, most couples are willing to take the risk of seeking to stimulate marital growth because they know that the alternative locks them into something less than they desire.

One of the purposes of this book is to teach you strategies for seeking marital growth that will help you initiate positive change. Following these strategies does not mean that you will experience no opposition to your efforts. It does mean that you are pursuing change in the most positive manner. The risks are minimal compared to the positive potential of moving your marriage to a more favorable season.

QUESTION

What if past hurts are so big (either within the marriage or from a spouse's family of origin) that a spouse is not able to address them even though motivated by a desire to improve the marriage? How can a couple begin to address a "worst case" marriage that is "below freezing" on the seasonal scale?

ANSWER

It is true that some people are in bondage to the emotional chains of the past. They wish things were different, but they don't have the emotional energy to take constructive steps. They read a book like The Four Seasons of Marriage *and dream that things could be better, but they are immobilized. Their minds are confused, their emotions are distorted, and giving up seems easier than trying. These people will almost always need a professional counselor, pastor, or mature friend to help them untangle the crossed wires of the past and find a way out of their hopelessness. Often, a trusted friend will be the one who encourages this person to seek professional counseling or other help that is needed. In this case, the friend is the lifeline between the troubled individual and the source of hope.*

QUESTION

Is it possible for a couple to live in two seasons at once, or does the worse season of the two define the marriage?

ANSWER

As we have noted in a previous chapter, the latter stages of fall and the beginning stages of winter may be hard to distinguish. Like-

wise, the last stages of spring and the first stages of summer tend to blend together. It is my belief that most marriages fit into one of the four seasons of marriage rather clearly. However, there is nothing wrong with describing your marriage as a fall/winter or a spring/summer marriage. It means that you have some of the characteristics of both seasons. The purpose of this book is to challenge couples to be always moving to a more favorable season of marriage or to continue living in such a season. We will not eliminate any of the four seasons from our marital experience. However, the ideal would be short falls and winters and long springs and summers. I believe that the strategies given in Part II of this book will help couples accomplish this ideal.

QUESTION

Is it necessary for both spouses to be in the same season in order for the marriage to be considered healthy and good?

ANSWER

In my opinion, a husband and wife are always in the same season of marriage, whether they realize it or not. It is certainly true that in my research I discovered couples who had different perceptions of the season of their marriage. I remember one husband who said, "We have a summer marriage; I could not be happier." But his wife said, "We are definitely in the winter stage of marriage. I feel so isolated from my husband." Whether he knew it or not, this man's marriage was in the winter season. His needs and expectations were apparently being met, but his wife's needs and expectations were a totally different story. If one spouse perceives a marriage to be in spring and the other spouse perceives it to be in summer, their differences are of little consequence, but when a couple is as far out of touch with each other as the couple I've described above, the marriage is definitely experiencing winter.

Because husbands and wives have different expectations about what a marriage ought to be, they also may have different percep-tions of the success of their marriage. Thus, it is not uncommon for a husband and wife to come to different conclusions about the season of their marriage. The reality of their marital relationship is proba-bly somewhere between their two differing perspectives, but what is important is that they communicate with each other. By using the information in The Four Seasons of Marriage, *they will be able to establish a meaningful dialogue that will bring them to a deeper understanding of each other and enhance the season of their mar-riage. (The Marital Seasons Profile located at the end of Part I can be extremely helpful in this communication process.)*

QUESTION

As couples move from one season to another, they will not always be in the same place or moving at the same pace. They won't always agree on what is happening in their marriage or what needs to happen. Is there more that can be said about how to work through these differences?

ANSWER

This question focuses on an important reality: We are individuals, and marriage does not erase our individuality. We interpret situa-tions differently. We have different emotional responses to the same experiences. We react differently to the events of life. For example, one spouse may process grief or disappointment by talking exces-sively, whereas his or her mate may withdraw in silent pain. Or one spouse works through adversity by activities while the other wants to gaze into the sunset and reflect. The object of marriage is not to make us clones of each other; rather it is for us to learn how to help our spouse develop his or her uniqueness so that together we can accomplish the purposes for which we were designed. When we see our spouse as a teammate rather than a competitor, we are far more likely to accomplish this objective. Rather than dividing over our differences, we come to delight in our differences—or what I call maximizing our differences.

❦

QUESTION

If I try one of the strategies in *The Four Seasons of Marriage* and it doesn't work, should I stop and try another?

ANSWER

As I see it, the strategies I have shared in this book are not to be followed sequentially. Neither are they independent projects to be completed one by one. Instead, they are lifestyle attitudes and behavior patterns that we should seek to build into the structure of our lives. For example, choosing a winning attitude is something we hope to develop for a lifetime, not just as a quick fix to shore up a weak season in our marriage. Speaking our spouse's love language is a never-ending but greatly rewarding way of life. Becoming an empathetic listener will serve you well at home, in the neighborhood, and at the office. Helping your spouse succeed is a lifetime project—and one that pays tremendous dividends! And learning to maximize your differences will make you and your spouse the winning team you desire to be.

Dealing with past failures may be a major first step toward a revitalized marriage, but you and your mate will forever need to deal with daily or weekly failures. Admitting that you've failed and asking for forgiveness will become a way of life. Likewise, you will forever have a positive or a negative influence on your spouse. It is my prayer that The Four Seasons of Marriage *will help you have a positive influence on your spouse.*

In my opinion, the strategies always work because they change our attitudes and actions, thus creating positive emotions. They may or may not stimulate complementary changes in your spouse. However, when both you and your spouse seek to live by these seven strategies, you will definitely spend more time in the spring and summer seasons of marriage.

QUESTION
So many of my friends are in the fall and winter seasons of marriage. What can I do to help them?

ANSWER
The concern that you express is what has motivated many couples to become involved in the marriage-enrichment movement over the past several years. Many others have devoted their vocational lives to marriage counseling. They deal with extremely troubled marriages, helping couples learn how to understand themselves and each other. Such counselors play an important role in preserving marriages.

Not every couple needs professional counseling, but every couple does need marriage enrichment. Marriages either grow or they regress. They are either moving toward (or deeper into) spring and summer, or they are moving toward (or deeper into) fall and winter. Exposing ourselves to the help that is available through the marriage-enrichment movement can make the difference between blooming crocuses and numbing ice storms.

That is why, over the past several years, I have devoted so much of my energy to writing books such as The Four Seasons of Marriage *and leading marriage seminars. I believe that many couples are healthy enough in their marriages that they can read a book and implement the concepts, thus experiencing marital growth. Others are auditory learners; they understand things best when they hear them explained. Thus the conference and seminar setting is an ideal format for these people. For many years, I have encouraged couples to attend a marriage-enrichment conference once a year and share a book on marriage once a year. If we can inspire widespread participation in these two approaches to marriage enrichment, I believe we will see thousands of marriages saved every year.*

I am encouraged that many communities and church organizations across the country are now offering small-group, marriage-enrichment activities. This trend offers great hope for the future. Finding out what is going on in your community and getting involved will not only help your marriage but will also enable you to help others.

181

If couples living in spring or summer marriages can reach out to those living in fall or winter and guide them to the appropriate marriage-enrichment opportunity, we can make a tremendous difference in the quality of marriages in this country. I know of nothing that has the potential to change the overall cultural climate more than enriched and growing marriages. When you work at improving the quality of your marriage, you influence not only your friends but also your children, grandchildren, and great-grandchildren for generations to come. The greatest thing you can do for your friends is to give them a model of a healthy marriage—a marriage that makes the most of the four seasons.

PART IV

The Four Seasons of Marriage Study Guide

Take a walk through town or a mall and you're sure to spot an older couple strolling hand in hand, their facial expressions and body language giving clear evidence of a quality of love that has gone the distance. What a rewarding feeling they must enjoy knowing they've beaten the odds; not only is their relationship still intact, but it's actually *thriving*. What does it take to have a marriage like that? What joys and struggles have they experienced along the way? We'd all like to know the secrets of their success.

Whether it has been years since your wedding day or only days since you returned from your honeymoon, one thing is certain: You are in the most special relationship two people can have. Sometimes, marriage may be a complete joy, whereas other times your life together may seem like an incurable disease. If you've been married for a while, your feelings have probably run the gamut between those two extremes.

All marriages experience the four seasons, including springtimes of vibrancy and excitement, fall seasons of discontentment and uncertainty, winters of anger and despair, and summertimes of growth and deepened love. Couples whose marriages survive—and thrive—have refused to give up, steadfastly sticking to the belief that their efforts to improve their marriages will eventually pay off.

The following study questions provide you and your spouse an opportunity to do some preventive maintenance on your relationship. They will help you learn more about each other, change some weak habits, discover new qualities to appreciate, and enhance the areas of attraction that first brought you together.

Because one of the more powerful ways to learn is by gleaning insights from others, the guide is designed for group discussions. However, it also includes personal questions that are ideal for spouses to work through together in private.

You'll also find ideas for dates with your mate. Most are simple and can be adapted to fit your circumstances. Discussion starters are included as an extra help.

Lastly, prayer topics will guide you as you commit your marriage to God in prayer. You are your spouse's most important prayer warrior. Praying together has the potential to bring huge blessings to your marriage.

Whether your marriage is basking in the summer sun or buried under drifts of winter snow, there's always room for greater fulfillment. May you thrive in the present season of your marriage, enriched by the history you share and overflowing with hope for the years to come.

THE NATURE OF MARRIAGE

"Each person is also endowed by God with certain latent possibilities. The partnership of marriage is an ideal environment for nurturing and developing these gifts and abilities."

1. Imagine a culture without marriage as a fundamental institution. Considering all aspects of culture—social, spiritual, financial, sexual, emotional, and generational—what benefits does monogamous marriage bring to society?

2. Many people, it seems, approach marriage as if it is a contract that can be broken if one party fails to uphold his or her end of the bargain or if the situation simply doesn't feel right anymore. The Bible, on the other hand, speaks of marriage as a *covenant* (Malachi 2:14). Discuss the differences between a contract and a covenant and the impact of those differences on a marriage. You may want to refer to a Bible dictionary or my book *Covenant Marriage: Building Communication and Intimacy.*

3. In the United States, divorce rates hover somewhere around 50 percent. What do you see as common causes for this unfortunate phenomenon? Consider cultural trends, various stresses from outside the marriage (jobs, relatives, schedules, media), and internal factors (character qualities, attitudes). What are some practical ways in which a couple can set up a hedge of protection around their relationship against divorce?

4. What does it mean to say that marriage is a *purposeful* relationship?

5. What does *intimacy* involve? How is it developed and maintained? What can threaten it?

6. "Emotions must lead to reason, and reason must be guided by truth if we are to take constructive action." Discuss the necessity of balancing emotions and reason. If you're willing, share with the group about a time in your marriage when your emotions got the best of you and dislodged reason. What was the effect on your spouse?

FOR COUPLES IN PRIVATE

Successful marriages are committed, united, intimate, purposeful, and complementary. On your own, list the personality traits that you and your spouse possess that complement each other. Then discuss your lists with each other. How do these traits strengthen, challenge, and benefit your relationship?

MAKE IT A DATE

If you and your spouse do not already have an established weekly date, it's time to start a new habit. Choose a mealtime that most easily fits your schedule and go to a favorite restaurant. Leave your cell phones, pagers, and other distractions at home, and focus on building your relationship.

CONVERSATION STARTERS

- Tell your spouse at least one quality you appreciate in him or her.
- Tell your spouse about an accomplishment that he or she has helped you achieve.

- Share prayer requests and commit to pray for each other this week.

COMMIT IT TO PRAYER

Be honest with each other about the season your marriage is in. Ask God to meet you in that season and to help you believe that he can restore, refresh, enhance, and invigorate your relationship. Challenge yourselves to pray together regularly.

WINTER

"Just as most people wouldn't lie down in the snow and wait to die, there's no reason to passively accept the coldness of a wintry marriage. There is a way out, and it begins with hope."

187

1. Discuss the characteristics and emotions of a winter marriage. Make a list of words and phrases that typify this season.
2. What brings most couples to the winter season of marriage? (Hint: It's a one-word answer.) Discuss how this factor can affect a marriage and how to avoid falling into this trap.
3. Most couples have experienced a winter season in their marriages or know couples who have. Keeping identities confidential, discuss relationship factors you have observed that contribute to a winter marriage.
4. How do "attitudes foster emotions"? How can choosing a positive attitude help a couple avoid or get out of the winter season?
5. What *actions* usually characterize a winter marriage?
6. Imagine that a friend has shared with you about the serious problems in his or her winter marriage. What can you say that would be helpful? What should you *not* say?

7. Read Matthew 13:15-16 aloud. What do these verses say about a hardened heart? What do these verses suggest about rigidity in a marriage? Consider the negative, snowballing effect of resentment in a relationship. Why is it necessary to deal first with a hardened heart before it's possible to heal a marriage?

8. Read Jeremiah 33:10-12 aloud. How might these verses offer hope to a troubled marriage?

9. "When two people choose to love again, the melting ice of winter will water the seeds of spring, and winter has served its ultimate purpose." Discuss the positive side of the winter season of marriage. What are some things you can do to move your marriage toward spring or to keep it from moving deeper into winter?

HOPE FOR THE WINTER SEASON OF MARRIAGE

My lover spoke and said to me, "Arise, my darling, my beautiful one, and come with me. See! The winter is past; the rains are over and gone. Flowers appear on the earth; the season of singing has come, the cooing of doves is heard in our land." SONG OF SONGS 2:10-12

On that day living water will flow out from Jerusalem, half to the eastern sea and half to the western sea, in summer and in winter. ZECHARIAH 14:8

Heal me, O Lord, and I will be healed; save me and I will be saved, for you are the one I praise. JEREMIAH 17:14

"I will heal their waywardness and love them freely, for my anger has turned away from them." HOSEA 14:4

Jesus said to him, "I will go and heal him." MATTHEW 8:7

My soul is in anguish. How long, O Lord, how long? Turn,

O LORD, AND DELIVER ME; SAVE ME BECAUSE OF YOUR UNFAILING
LOVE.   PSALM 6:3-4

I HAVE TAKEN AN OATH AND CONFIRMED IT, THAT I WILL FOLLOW
YOUR RIGHTEOUS LAWS. I HAVE SUFFERED MUCH; PRESERVE MY LIFE,
O LORD, ACCORDING TO YOUR WORD. ACCEPT, O LORD, THE
WILLING PRAISE OF MY MOUTH, AND TEACH ME YOUR LAWS.
PSALM 119:106-108

FOR COUPLES IN PRIVATE
No matter what the current state of your marriage is, most
likely you've experienced a time with your spouse that was joyful. After brainstorming on your own, make a list of positive
things you have learned from your spouse. If you're in a winter
season, this may require some hard work, but it can be a valuable part of reestablishing a loving foundation on which to
build your relationship. Share your list with your spouse.

MAKE IT A DATE
Do something lighthearted together. Rent a favorite comedy
DVD, play a board game, stroll through a park, or volunteer for
a service project.

CONVERSATION STARTERS
   • Set a positive tone by talking about the highlights of your week.
   • Update each other on family members, work issues, or
      neighborhood happenings.
   • Talk about your relationship, but for every area you bring
      up that needs improvement, mention two things you value
      about your relationship or your spouse. In positive terms,
      discuss why you want to work on a particular part of your
      marriage.

• Exchange prayer requests and commit to pray for each other and for your relationship this week.

COMMIT IT TO PRAYER

Focus on your spouse's needs as you pray for your marriage. As much as you might be tempted to pour out your own feelings, pray instead about what is important to your spouse. Ask God to help you see your spouse through God's eyes.

❧

SPRING

"Change is perceived as an opportunity for new beginnings, and springtime couples fully expect to make the best of those opportunities."

1. Discuss the characteristics and emotions of a spring marriage. Make a list of words and phrases that typify this season.
2. Share with the group about a spring season from your marriage. How long did it last? What events prompted its beginning? its end?
3. Discuss how other areas of life—such as careers, children, relatives, health, or finances—can affect a spring season for better or worse. Consider potential threats to a spring marriage as well as events that can enhance the season.
4. "Because we are creatures of choice, we can create new beginnings whenever we desire." This sounds good, but let's get practical. What specific choices in attitudes and actions can we make to turn a fall or winter marriage into a

spring marriage (or protect a spring marriage already in full swing)?

5. Coping with a fading spring can be difficult for an unprepared couple who thought the season would last forever. If you're willing, share insights about how you've dealt with the change of seasons in your marriage or what you've observed in other marriages.

6. "Even in the springtime, there can be difficulties, but the prevailing attitude is one of anticipated growth rather than despair." Discuss the importance of attitude and behavior in establishing or maintaining a springtime marriage. What can you do to make some positive adjustments in this regard in your own marriage?

7. An "attitude of gratitude" characterizes spring marriages. What is the value of maintaining a spirit of thankfulness about your spouse?

8. Read Psalms 28:7 and 62:8 aloud. How does trusting God teach us to imitate his trustworthiness? How does God's trustworthiness enable us to take the risk of trusting someone else?

9. Discuss the downside of the spring season of marriage. What are some things you can do to keep spring alive?

ENCOURAGEMENT FOR THE SPRING SEASON OF MARRIAGE
O LORD ALMIGHTY, BLESSED IS THE MAN WHO TRUSTS IN YOU.
PSALM 84:12

I PRAY THAT OUT OF HIS GLORIOUS RICHES HE MAY STRENGTHEN YOU WITH POWER THROUGH HIS SPIRIT IN YOUR INNER BEING, SO THAT CHRIST MAY DWELL IN YOUR HEARTS THROUGH FAITH. AND I PRAY THAT YOU, BEING ROOTED AND ESTABLISHED IN LOVE, MAY HAVE POWER, TOGETHER WITH ALL THE SAINTS, TO GRASP HOW WIDE AND

LONG AND HIGH AND DEEP IS THE LOVE OF CHRIST, AND TO KNOW
THIS LOVE THAT SURPASSES KNOWLEDGE—THAT YOU MAY BE
FILLED TO THE MEASURE OF ALL THE FULLNESS OF GOD.
EPHESIANS 3:16-19

AND SO WE KNOW AND RELY ON THE LOVE GOD HAS FOR US. GOD IS
LOVE. WHOEVER LIVES IN LOVE LIVES IN GOD, AND GOD IN HIM.
1 JOHN 4:16

FOR THE LORD YOUR GOD WILL BLESS YOU IN ALL YOUR HARVEST
AND IN ALL THE WORK OF YOUR HANDS, AND YOUR JOY WILL BE
COMPLETE. DEUTERONOMY 16:15

THE LORD IS MY STRENGTH AND MY SHIELD; MY HEART TRUSTS IN
HIM, AND I AM HELPED. MY HEART LEAPS FOR JOY AND I WILL GIVE
THANKS TO HIM IN SONG.   PSALM 28:7

IN ALL MY PRAYERS FOR ALL OF YOU, I ALWAYS PRAY WITH JOY.
PHILIPPIANS 1:4

FOR COUPLES IN PRIVATE
Stroll down memory lane together as you discuss memories of a
spring season in your relationship. What about that season
made you feel secure and joyful in your love for each other?
Talk about areas you'd like to see improved and changes you
can make to renew the springtime in your marriage.

MAKE IT A DATE
Spread God's love and get refilled in the process: Spend a couple of hours volunteering at a soup kitchen or helping a neigh-
bor in need. Serving others can enrich your relationship and
offer a fresh look at how you have been blessed.

CONVERSATION STARTERS
  • Update each other on the events of the week, on happen-
    ings at work and home, and about the kids (if applicable).

- Talk about some of the blessings in your lives.
- Exchange prayer requests and commit to pray for each other and for your relationship this week.

COMMIT IT TO PRAYER

Focus on gratitude! Spend a few minutes thanking God together for bringing you to where you are today and for offering his strength to deal with the circumstances he allows in your lives. Thank God for the ways in which your personality complements and challenges your spouse, and ask him to remind you throughout the week of reasons to be grateful for your marriage and for your spouse.

SUMMER

"If our marriage is in the season of summer, we will share a deep sense of commitment and satisfaction. And we will feel secure in each other's love. . . . Summer does not equal perfection, but it does mean that couples in this season have a sense of accomplishment and a desire to keep growing."

1. Discuss the characteristics and emotions of a summer marriage. Make a list of words and phrases that typify this season.
2. Explain your understanding of *constructive communication*. What makes communication effective? Share your ideas about the importance of communication and what happens when it's lacking in a relationship.
3. Talk about various forms of nonverbal communication and

how they can be beneficial (or can add confusion) to a situation.

4. Jeremy and Ruth made some "extra" vows to each other when they got married (see page 40). Discuss any general guidelines that you and your spouse established for your life together that weren't part of the traditional wedding vows. Are there any guidelines you'd like to establish now that you understand the characteristics of a summer marriage?

5. "Couples who desire to continue in the summer season will consciously give each other the freedom to think, feel, and react differently." Discuss the importance of accepting each other's differences. If you're willing, share about a time you either succeeded or failed at this and how you and your spouse were able to move on to a greater understanding of each other.

6. How can our differences refine us? Read Proverbs 27:17, Mark 9:49-50, and Colossians 3:15. Describe what a relationship would look like if two people had identical personalities. How would the relationship be weakened?

7. Discuss with the group any books, video series, or seminars you've found helpful in developing your marriage. What did you gain from these tools?

8. What role has spiritual growth played in your marriage? What benefits have accrued as a result of your faith? Describe a couple whose marriage you respect because of their faith. What are the evidences of their faith in their marriage relationship?

9. Discuss the downside of the summer season of marriage. What are some things you can do to "water" your relationship and keep it growing, fresh, and vibrant?

GROWTH FOR THE SUMMER SEASON OF MARRIAGE

Do not repay anyone evil for evil. Be careful to do what is right in the eyes of everybody. If it is possible, as far as it depends on you, live at peace with everyone.
ROMANS 12:17-18

Aim for perfection, listen to my appeal, be of one mind, live in peace. And the God of love and peace will be with you.
2 CORINTHIANS 13:11

This is how we know what love is: Jesus Christ laid down his life for us. And we ought to lay down our lives for our brothers. If anyone has material possessions and sees his brother in need but has no pity on him, how can the love of God be in him? Dear children, let us not love with words or tongue but with actions and in truth.
1 JOHN 3:16-18

Whoever lives in love lives in God, and God in him. In this way, love is made complete among us. We love because he first loved us.   1 JOHN 4:16-17, 19

No discipline seems pleasant at the time, but painful. Later on, however, it produces a harvest of righteousness and peace for those who have been trained by it.   HEBREWS 12:11

FOR COUPLES IN PRIVATE

Talk with your spouse about the ways you communicate. What topics tend to dominate your conversations? What else would you like to talk about? Discuss what you learn from your spouse's nonverbal communication.

MAKE IT A DATE

Commemorate the growth in your marriage in a tangible way by planting something together. It might be an herb or vegetable garden, a simple houseplant, a shrub, or a flowering tree.

Each time you look at it, you'll be reminded to nurture your relationship. Years down the road, you'll be able to enjoy the growth of your plant(s) and your relationship.

CONVERSATION STARTERS

- Jump-start your conversation by deciding together what you'd like to plant. Discuss the reasons for your choice.
- How have you changed since meeting your spouse? How has your spouse changed? What drew you to each other in the beginning? What qualities that you might not have seen at first have you come to appreciate?
- How have your differences created challenges for your relationship? How have they benefited your relationship?
- Exchange prayer requests and commit to pray for each other and for your relationship this week.

COMMIT IT TO PRAYER

Focus your prayer time on growth. Choose one or two specific areas of your life together that you'd like to surrender to God. Ask God for strength and patience as you work together to pursue spiritual growth.

FALL

"It takes both spouses to move a marriage from fall to spring, but it takes only one to move from fall to winter. The way we think and the actions we take make all the difference."

1. Discuss the characteristics and emotions of a fall marriage. Make a list of words and phrases that typify this season.

2. Recall a time when you felt either discouraged or downright depressed about something in your life (not necessarily stemming from your marriage). How did that event affect your attitudes, feelings, and actions about other areas of your life? Discuss the effects on your marriage of ongoing stress (physical, emotional, mental, spiritual, social, financial). What are some avenues of help for getting through tough times?

3. As a group, spend time sharing favorite Scripture passages that offer hope for dealing with the fall season of marriage. Make a group list for each member to keep handy. Here's a couple to get you started: Psalm 16:8-9; Psalm 31:23-24.

4. Read Psalm 42 aloud. Make a list of words, phrases, and concepts that offer hope in God's power to repair struggling marriages.

5. It's a cliché that change is inevitable, but there's no denying that it's true. Discuss the positive and negative aspects of change, including good and not-so-good habits of dealing with change.

6. Fear is one of the emotions often experienced in a fall marriage. Talk about the destructive forces of fear on individuals and relationships. What are some things that people commonly fear? When does fear become a negative hang-up instead of simply a concern? How does fear devalue the Lord's power and goodness?

7. Complete the following sentence and discuss it with your group: "Without a doubt, the number one contributor to the fall season of marriage—overwhelmingly—is the action of _____, or taking no action at all."

8. Nurturing common interests is one way to avoid neglecting your spouse. Is it easy for you and your spouse to come up

197

with activities you both enjoy? What have you done to discover mutual interests? How can couples overcome the unsettling realization that they don't seem to have much in common? How is faith a bond that unites people regardless of their personalities or interests?

9. Discuss the positive side of the fall season of marriage. What are some things you can do to move your marriage toward spring or to keep it from moving toward winter?

LIFELINES FOR THE FALL SEASON OF MARRIAGE

[LOVE] ALWAYS PROTECTS, ALWAYS TRUSTS, ALWAYS HOPES, ALWAYS PERSEVERES.   1 CORINTHIANS 13:7

OUT OF THE MOST SEVERE TRIAL, THEIR OVERFLOWING JOY AND THEIR EXTREME POVERTY WELLED UP IN RICH GENEROSITY. 2 CORINTHIANS 8:2

THIS IS HOW GOD SHOWED HIS LOVE AMONG US: HE SENT HIS ONE AND ONLY SON INTO THE WORLD THAT WE MIGHT LIVE THROUGH HIM. THIS IS LOVE: NOT THAT WE LOVED GOD, BUT THAT HE LOVED US AND SENT HIS SON AS AN ATONING SACRIFICE FOR OUR SINS. DEAR FRIENDS, SINCE GOD SO LOVED US, WE ALSO OUGHT TO LOVE ONE ANOTHER.   1 JOHN 4:9-11

DO NOT LET YOUR HEART ENVY SINNERS, BUT ALWAYS BE ZEALOUS FOR THE FEAR OF THE LORD. THERE IS SURELY A FUTURE HOPE FOR YOU, AND YOUR HOPE WILL NOT BE CUT OFF. LISTEN, MY SON, AND BE WISE, AND KEEP YOUR HEART ON THE RIGHT PATH. PROVERBS 23:17-19

HE WHO WAS SEATED ON THE THRONE SAID, "I AM MAKING EVERY-THING NEW!" THEN HE SAID, "WRITE THIS DOWN, FOR THESE WORDS ARE TRUSTWORTHY AND TRUE."   REVELATION 21:5

A GENEROUS MAN WILL PROSPER; HE WHO REFRESHES OTHERS WILL HIMSELF BE REFRESHED.   PROVERBS 11:25

FOR THIS IS WHAT THE HIGH AND LOFTY ONE SAYS—HE WHO LIVES
FOREVER, WHOSE NAME IS HOLY: "I LIVE IN A HIGH AND HOLY PLACE,
BUT ALSO WITH HIM WHO IS CONTRITE AND LOWLY IN SPIRIT, TO
REVIVE THE SPIRIT OF THE LOWLY AND TO REVIVE THE HEART OF THE
CONTRITE." ISAIAH 57:15

FOR COUPLES IN PRIVATE

Discuss your individual fears, whether or not those fears center
on your marriage. Talk about the role that faith has played in
your relationship and the role you'd like for it to have in the
future. Discuss specific things you can do to ease each other's
fears, lessen each other's daily burdens, and boost each other's
self-esteem.

MAKE IT A DATE

Discover new areas of common interest. Go out for dessert, or
curl up on the couch together, and make a list of all your interests. Begin by brainstorming—together—as many of each
spouse's interests as possible. This activity may very well awaken
a new awareness of what motivates each of you. Use the same
process to create two lists of your dreams for the future, which
may include experiences you'd like to have at some point in life.
Your list might include such things as backpacking through the
Australian outback, learning to play the piano, organizing your
closet, or buying a dog. Commit to help your spouse achieve at
least one of his or her dreams. Also, commit to take part in at
least one of his or her favorite interests in the next month.

CONVERSATION STARTERS

- Update each other on the events of the week, on happen-
  ings at work and home, and about the kids (if applicable).
- Talk about your faith. What are you currently enjoying

about your relationship with God? What questions would you like to ask him someday?

- Choose one of your spouse's positive character strengths and explain why you appreciate it.
- Exchange prayer requests and commit to pray for each other and for your relationship this week.

COMMIT IT TO PRAYER

Spend a few minutes praying together about the things that trigger fear and insecurity. Ask God to build stability and security in your marriage and to help you find more areas of common interest. Ask God to help you grow in appreciation for those interests of your spouse's that you don't necessarily share.

❧

MARITAL SEASONS PROFILE

"Every couple will experience a succession of winters, summers, springs, and falls. . . . Regardless of the season of your marriage, there's hope and there's room for improvement."

FOR COUPLES IN PRIVATE

Set aside enough time to work through the profiles and spend time discussing your responses. Revisit the book section for direction on proceeding through the profile. Talk about areas of difference in your responses. Are you on the same page as far as your feelings about your relationship? Why or why not? Choose five words from the profile chart that hit you the most powerfully. Explain what each one means to you. If most are negative, choose a sixth one that's positive to add a tone of hope to your discussion. If your spouse is willing, pray together about the concerns or blessings revealed by the profile.

FOR GROUP DISCUSSION

Share thoughts within your group regarding the profile. Allow for a broad range of disclosure—some members may want to talk a lot, whereas others may not feel as comfortable.

1. Were the profile results in line with how you've been feeling recently about your marriage? If not, how did they differ?
2. Which words in the profile stood out to you the most? Which ones bothered you? Which ones brought a smile?
3. Was the profile helpful in prompting discussion with your spouse?
4. Take time to encourage each couple in the group. Highlight specific strengths you see in each person and discuss how those strengths can enhance his or her marriage. This step may be especially helpful for couples in the fall and winter seasons, who may be feeling discouraged by their profile results. Affirmation from others can go a long way toward helping them see the value of persevering in their relationship.

PART II

*Seven Strategies to Enhance
the Seasons of Your Marriage*

STRATEGY 1: DEAL WITH PAST FAILURES

*"Dealing with past failures often clears the debris in a relationship
and paves the way for implementing the other strategies."*

---

1. Why is it important to deal with past issues before moving forward? What might be some consequences of not addressing those issues? If you're willing, share a positive or negative personal experience.
2. Of the three steps involved in dealing with the past—identifying past failures, confession and repentance, and forgiveness—which have you found to be the most difficult? Why?
3. Why is it important to look at our own failures first when dealing with past hurts? Consider what the Bible says about this. Look up the following verses and summarize the insights they offer:
   • Psalm 50:6
   • Lamentations 3:58-59
   • Zechariah 7:9
   • Matthew 7:2-5
   • Romans 2:1-7

4. Read Psalm 78:1-8. What are some potential benefits of working through past issues?

5. Ecclesiastes 3:15 says, "God will call the past to account." Discuss how this truth works together with Isaiah 43:18: "Forget the former things; do not dwell on the past."

6. Read Isaiah 43:19-21, 25. What truths and hope do these verses offer to a spouse who is hurting? What characteristics of God can we rely on to see us through difficult times?

7. It isn't always easy to let go of hurts; in fact, sometimes it's very difficult. Love, however, "keeps no record of wrongs" (1 Corinthians 13:5). In practical, day-to-day living, what does it mean to keep no record of wrongs? Does it mean that we no longer feel the pain? How much continued discussion should be "allowed" regarding the hurt?

8. Share about the difficulties or resistance you may feel about focusing on your own mistakes in your marriage.

9. While communicating with your spouse, have you developed the habit of using "I felt . . ." examples instead of "You made me feel . . ." accusations? Discuss the power of the "I felt . . ." method for diffusing tension and defensiveness. If possible, share a personal example.

10. Read Psalm 51 aloud. How do King David's heart attitude and words challenge you?

11. Discuss the three benefits of dealing with past failures.

MAKE IT A DATE

Much of the focus of this section has been on dealing with negative aspects from the past. However, for most couples, the past holds joy as well. Revisit a favorite place or a positive memory from your past as a couple. You could go back to the location of your first date, listen to "your song," or curl up on the couch for a cozy evening of discussing only your favorite memories of your life together. Remind yourselves of why you fell in love.

CONVERSATION STARTERS
- Talk about your first date, including where you went, what you did, how you felt. Remember as many details as you can.
- Talk about how you've grown as individuals and as a couple since then.
- Exchange prayer requests and commit to pray for each other and for your relationship this week.

❧

STRATEGY 2: CHOOSE A WINNING ATTITUDE

"What we think largely influences what we do. In turn, our actions greatly influence our emotions. This connection between attitude and actions opens a door of hope for all couples. If we can change our thinking, we can change the season of our marriage."

1. "The most common mistake couples make is allowing negative emotions to dictate their behavior." Discuss this idea with your group.
2. "It is not what happens to us but how we *interpret* what happens to us (our attitude) that makes the difference between success and failure." Share about a situation overcoming extreme difficulties that you've experienced or observed. How did attitude affect the outcome?
3. Discuss the five characteristics of a Christian worldview and how they foster a positive attitude.

4. How is an attitude based on who a person is more productive than one based on his or her actions?

5. Describe your role in your spouse's life. How can reminding yourself of your role encourage you to maintain a positive attitude toward your spouse?

6. Summarize and discuss the five steps that break the cycle of negativity.

7. Read Psalms 69 and 102 aloud. How did the writer's attitude shift from the beginning to the end? What example does that set for us?

8. Read Romans 14:17-19. How can these verses be applied in a marriage relationship?

9. Although we can't change people directly, how can our actions influence them? Share about a time when you either influenced someone or were influenced by someone and your attitude or behavior changed as a result.

10. Why is choosing a good attitude often difficult? How can we find the strength to overcome those difficult barriers?

FOR COUPLES IN PRIVATE

On your own this week, write down a few qualities about your spouse that make him or her special to God. Then write down a few thoughts about your role in his or her life. Each time you catch yourself grumbling about something your spouse said or did, remind yourself to focus on the things you wrote down. Commit yourself to establishing a grateful attitude.

❦

STRATEGY 3: LEARN TO SPEAK YOUR SPOUSE'S LOVE LANGUAGE

"Nothing holds more potential for changing the season of your marriage than learning the truth about love."

───────────────

1. "Our culture is largely ignorant of the true nature of love and its effect on human relationships." Discuss modern culture's views of love. How is love portrayed in the media?

2. Talk about the concept of a "love tank." This may be a new idea for some people in the group. Spend a few minutes sharing thoughts about the role that spouses play in filling each other's love tank.

3. What characteristics are recognizable in a person whose love tank is empty? full? How are other areas of life (parenting, career, self-esteem, ministry) affected by an empty (or a full) love tank?

4. Describe *emotional obsession* and its role in developing love. What is the average duration of this stage?

5. What are the benefits of the first, euphoric stage of love? What is the downside?

6. Describe the second, more intentional, phase of love. What are the pros and cons of this stage?

7. Read 1 Corinthians 13 aloud. What key words, phrases, and concepts show that love is *intentional?* Spend some time discussing how to foster these qualities.

8. How does withdrawing in anger reap negative results?

9. Briefly define and discuss the five love languages. Are these "languages" true to life for members of the group?

10. Discuss each group member's love language, as well as how it was identified. The added insight from others in the group can often help members who are having trouble figuring out which language is theirs.

11. If you're willing, share when and how you and your spouse discovered each other's love language and how your relationship was affected by expressing love in those ways.

COMMIT IT TO PRAYER

Spend time praying together for insight and patience to learn to speak your spouse's love language. Thank God for each other, expressing specific qualities or habits for which you are grateful. Loving others in their "native language" may bring us out of our comfort zones, but when we are obeying God's command to love each other, he will give us the tools we need to accomplish it.

STRATEGY 4: DEVELOP THE AWESOME POWER OF EMPATHETIC LISTENING

"Open communication is the lifeblood that keeps a marriage in the spring and summer seasons. Conversely, failure to communicate is what brings on fall and winter."

1. What does *empathy* mean? What does empathetic listening encourage and why?

2. Describe the atmosphere of a relationship that has a successful history of empathetic listening. What do we sabotage by failing to listen empathetically?

3. What is involved in the shift from *egocentric* to *empathetic* listening? Read James 1:19 and Philippians 2:3 aloud and apply them to your answers.

4. Describe the difference between *perceptions* and *feelings*. Which of these are we more likely to observe or understand? Why is it important to understand *both* in our spouses? Discuss how your listening skills can affect your spouse's self-esteem.

5. What are some reasons why people are noncommunicative?

6. Discuss the differences between Dead Sea people and Babbling Brooks. What are the strengths and weaknesses of each type? Which one describes you? Which one describes your spouse? What do Deuteronomy 32:2, Proverbs 10:19, Proverbs 15:1, 4, and Philippians 2:4 say about talking too much?

7. Read Isaiah 42:2-3. Discuss how Jesus set the example for communicating in a healing way.

8. Define and discuss the four aspects of learning to listen empathetically (see pages 107-118). Which one is typically the most difficult for you? Why?

9. Do you ever catch yourself believing that your viewpoints are usually the most accurate and that those of others are wrong? What feelings does it evoke in you when others seem to think they are always right?

10. Role-play in the group at least one positive example of how to affirm someone even when his or her opinions differ from yours.

11. What is the "capstone of empathetic listening"? Why is this important?

12. Read aloud the fourteen steps involved in learning empathetic listening. Steps 10-12 focus on clarifying and summarizing your spouse's ideas and emotions. Why is it important to give feedback regarding your understanding of your spouse's communication?

13. "When [couples] seek to resolve—rather than win—an argument, they not only discover workable solutions but also find intimacy with their spouse." Discuss how you've seen this work in your marriage (or in someone else's).

FOR COUPLES IN PRIVATE

Practice empathetic listening together as you discuss a topic of your choice. (If possible, choose something nonconfrontational for this practice session.) Look through the newspaper or watch a current events program on TV. Choose a current cultural event or trend and discuss your opinions about it. Employ the listening, reflecting, and affirming skills you've learned from this strategy. Give your spouse feedback about how well you felt understood.

❦

STRATEGY 5: DISCOVER THE JOY OF HELPING YOUR SPOUSE SUCCEED

"A successful wife is one who expends her time and energy helping her husband reach his potential for God and for doing good in the world. Likewise, a successful husband is one who helps his wife succeed."

———————

1. Take time to hear each group member's definition of *success*.
2. Discuss the following statement about spouses serving each other: "A truly great husband is one who is willing to serve his wife. A truly great wife is one who is willing to serve her husband. If you want to breathe new life into a fall or winter marriage, start serving your spouse." If you're willing, share how your spouse serves you and how that makes you feel loved.
3. How does human nature make it difficult for us to serve others? Is the typical societal definition of *success* based on power or love? Explain your answer.
4. As you seek to grow in serving your spouse, why is it important to begin on a spiritual level by asking God for help?
5. Review the "three simple questions to help your spouse succeed." What keeps you from asking your spouse these questions?
6. What do a person's complaints reveal?
7. What are four practical ways to help your spouse succeed?

211

8. Read aloud Proverbs 12:25, Proverbs 25:11, Romans 15:5, and 1 Thessalonians 5:11. Discuss your definition of *encouragement.*

9. If you're willing, share how your spouse has helped you succeed at something.

10. Brainstorm some practical things you can say to a spouse who has a dream that you see as unrealistic. How do you support your spouse as a *person,* regardless of his or her *dream?*

11. Read aloud Ephesians 6:7 and Colossians 3:23. What do these verses say about our attitude toward helping our spouses?

12. Discuss the pros and cons of emotions and how God intends for our emotions "to be motivational instruments that move us in a positive direction."

13. "Respect does not indicate that you agree on everything, but it does mean that you give your spouse the freedom to be an individual." Discuss how this works in a marriage. How can respect strengthen your spouse and your relationship?

14. Brainstorm some healthy and respectful ways to express disappointment in someone's actions.

MAKE IT A DATE

This date is all about serving and showing respect for your spouse. It requires a bit of pre-date planning. Sometime during the week before the date, ask your spouse for two errands or tasks that you can do to serve him or her—and then do them. During your date time, communicate with each other how those acts of service made each of you feel loved and understood. Nurture each other's success and help each other thrive through your actions and words.

CONVERSATION STARTERS

- Update your spouse on how your week is going, and discuss ways in which you can help each other succeed.
- Discuss the following statement: "To show respect is to look for your mate's God-given *giftedness* and to affirm and encourage his or her uniqueness."
- Verbalize some of the God-given gifts you value in your spouse.
- Exchange prayer requests and commit to pray for each other and for your relationship this week.

※

STRATEGY 6: MAXIMIZE YOUR DIFFERENCES

"After thirty years of counseling married couples, I am convinced there are no irreconcilable differences, only people who refuse to reconcile. . . . When each spouse recognizes and affirms the other's uniqueness, the differences themselves weld the couple into an unbeatable team."

1. Poll the group to find out how many couples are cases of "opposites attract."
2. What are the five steps for maximizing differences in marriage? Briefly discuss each one.
3. If couples are willing, ask husbands and wives to share a mild irritation (something their spouse does) and then answer the following two questions: Why do these things irritate me? What differences do these irritations reveal?
4. "In most cases, the reason you get irritated is because your

spouse doesn't do something the way you would do it."
Discuss how this idea corresponds to our human tendency
to be egocentric.

5. Read aloud the list of common differences between
husbands and wives on page 138. Which of these characterize you and your spouse?

6. Discuss the idea that "every difference has a positive side."
Share one difference of which you and your spouse have
discovered the positive side. What was the process of learning to appreciate that difference? (Your response to this
question may provide encouragement for others.)

7. Imagine a marriage in which spouses stifle their differences
to "keep the peace." How can this have negative results and
actually destroy growth and peace?

8. How can facing our differences cause fear or hesitation
in us?

9. Discuss marriages you've observed (perhaps your own) in
which the spouses maximize their differences. Contrast these
examples with marriages you've observed (or perhaps your
own) where the spouses' differences are allowed to weaken
the relationship. How do these relational dynamics affect
each spouse in the marriage, as well as in other areas of life
(parenting, friendships, jobs, ministry)?

10. Read Romans 14:19, Ephesians 4:29, and 2 Timothy 2:24.
Discuss how these truths offer wisdom for maximizing our
differences.

COMMIT IT TO PRAYER

Spend time alone praying about your spouse's habits or actions
that irritate you. Ask God to reveal what those irritations show
about you, your spouse, and your relationship. Ask God to help

you develop patience; trust him to show you practical ways to appreciate and maximize your differences with your spouse. Pray with your spouse about your differences, and commit yourselves to allowing God to use your complementary characteristics for his work and purposes.

❧

STRATEGY 7: IMPLEMENT THE POWER OF POSITIVE INFLUENCE

"Thousands of people live in these self-made prisons because they fail to understand the power of positive influence. It is true that you cannot change your spouse, but it is equally true that you can and do influence your spouse every day. . . . When a husband or wife is willing to choose a positive attitude that leads to positive actions, the change in the spouse is often radical."

1. Do you have a story of how you changed as a result of someone else's influence? Have you seen someone change because of your influence? Share with the group.
2. What is the difference between being an *influencer* and a *manipulator*?
3. How do most people react when they feel manipulated?
4. What does manipulation communicate about a person's self-esteem? honesty? pride?
5. Read Psalm 120:3-4 and 1 Peter 2:1. How is manipulation deceitful? Based on these verses, how does God feel about deception?
6. Discuss the idea that we don't have to be controlled by

emotions, whether our own or our spouse's. When is it difficult to apply that concept? What are some helpful tips to putting it into practice in daily life?

7. Discuss with the group various positive choices you've made—from trivial to crucial—that went against your feelings at the time.

8. What is the first step in any positive change? Discuss the idea that "positive choices lead to positive actions that result in positive feelings."

9. What value is there in admitting your feelings but not being controlled by them?

10. Skim 1 Samuel 1–2, the story of Hannah's desire for a child. Describe her emotions, how she dealt with them, and how she became a person of influence in positive rather than negative ways.

COMMIT IT TO PRAYER

This strategy is appropriate when your spouse does not show interest in working on your marriage. The greatest tool at your disposal is prayer. Whatever season your marriage is in, bring God's loving power into your marriage. Talk to him about your hurts, failures, doubts, and joys. He is your ally and your source of strength. Ask him to help you gain control over your emotions; he will also give you the ability to keep from being controlled by your spouse's emotions. Ask God for wisdom and discernment in choosing positive attitudes, words, and actions.

PART III

Putting Your Plan into Practice

MOVING FORWARD FROM HERE AND NOW

1. What is one key truth you gained from this book? this study? the group discussions?
2. Which strategy spoke to you the most? Which strategy spoke the most to your spouse?
3. Have you been able to apply any of the strategies in your marriage yet? If so, share what you've done and the results.
4. Have you and your spouse shared any meaningful moments through the Make It a Date, For Couples in Private, or Commit It to Prayer suggestions? If you're willing, share a highlight or two with the group.
5. What goals have you set on your own or with your spouse for the coming months? What steps will you take to implement them?

WORDS OF HOPE IN CLOSING

> *"When a husband and wife both live according to God's design for them, they will be mutually submitted to each other and looking out for each other's best interest. In this free and loving partnership, they will be able to accomplish the purpose that God has for their life together. God designed just such a marriage for you. . . . I have seen these strategies turn literally thousands of marriages from the coldness of*

winter to the excitement of spring. I know they will work for you."

I pray that out of his glorious riches he may strengthen you with power through his Spirit in your inner being, so that Christ may dwell in your hearts through faith. And I pray that you, being rooted and established in love, may have power, together with all the saints, to grasp how wide and long and high and deep is the love of Christ, and to know this love that surpasses knowledge—that you may be filled to the measure of all the fullness of God. (Ephesians 3:16-20)

You've made it this far in your marriage. Keep going. There is no way to know the miraculous power of God if we quit before he is finished working. And he *is* working all the time, you can count on that. He has wonderful blessings ahead for you and your spouse. May you become one of those older couples that inspire the thought, *Wow, they've gone the distance!*

NOTES

THE NATURE OF MARRIAGE

1. Kim McAlister, "The X Generation," *HR* magazine, 39 (May, 1994): 21.
2. Genesis 2:24.
3. Genesis 2:18.
4. Ecclesiastes 4:9-10.

WINTER

1. James 1:2-4.
2. Romans 8:28-29.
3. 1 Peter 4:8.

SUMMER

1. For more information on these weekend getaways, visit www.lifeway.com/events or call (800) 254-2022.
2. Two good books that discuss the connection between a couple's faith and the quality of their marriage are *The Case for Marriage* by Linda J. Waite and Maggie Gallagher (New York: Doubleday, 2000) and *Why Marriage Matters* by Glenn T. Stanton (Colorado Springs: Pinon Press, 1997).

STRATEGY 1

1. My comments are based on what Jesus says about forgiveness in Matthew 6:14-15;18:35.

STRATEGY 3

1. Dorothy Tennov, *Love and Limerance* (New York: Stein and Day, 1979), 142.
2. For more information on the five love languages, see Gary Chapman, *The Five Love Languages* (Chicago: Northfield, 2004).

STRATEGY 4

1. Paul Tournier, *To Understand Each Other*, John S. Gilmour, trans. (Atlanta: John Knox, 1967), 4.

STRATEGY 5

1. Harold J. Sala, *Something More Than Love* (Denver: Accent, 1983), 105.
2. Acts 10:38.
3. John 13:14-15, 17.
4. Matthew 20:26.
5. Sala, *Something More Than Love*, 103.

6. Romans 12:15 (author's paraphrase).
7. Genesis 2:18.

STRATEGY 6

1. Genesis 2:24.
2. Many couples have found it helpful to take a basic personality test such as the *Myers-Briggs Personality Inventory.* Your local counselor can help you locate such an inventory if you are interested.
3. Leviticus 23:3.
4. Ecclesiastes 3:1-11.
5. 2 Thessalonians 3:10.
6. Proverbs 19:15; 31:27.

STRATEGY 7

1. Matthew 7:5.
2. Viktor E. Frankl, *Man's Search for Meaning* (New York: Washington Square Books, 1984), 86.

THE FOUR SEASONS
FICTION SERIES

by Dr. Gary Chapman & Catherine Palmer

Based on *The Four Seasons of Marriage* by Gary Chapman, this new fiction series takes a lighthearted look at common marital challenges. In Deepwater Cove, you'll meet quirky neighbors, see struggles you've faced, and come to realize that—even when it comes to marriage—winter won't last forever!

TYNDALE FICTION

Introducing the

CHAPMAN GUIDES

Simple solutions to life's most difficult problems

EVERYBODY WINS

The Chapman Guide to
Solving Conflicts Without Arguing

CONFLICT IS INEVITABLE.
ARGUING IS A CHOICE.

Relationship expert Dr. Gary Chapman provides a simple blueprint to help you and your spouse find win-win solutions to everyday disagreements and leave both of you feeling loved, listened to, and appreciated.

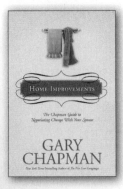

HOME IMPROVEMENTS

The Chapman Guide to
Negotiating Change With Your Spouse

IS YOUR SPOUSE'S BEHAVIOR
DRIVING YOU CRAZY?

Over time, annoying little habits can wreak havoc on a relationship. After years of counseling battle-weary couples, Dr. Gary Chapman has developed a simple and effective approach that will help you and your spouse turn those irritating behaviors around once and for all.

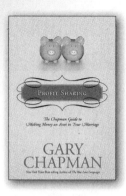

PROFIT SHARING

The Chapman Guide to
Making Money an Asset in Your Marriage

WHEN YOURS AND MINE BECOME OURS.

Money is often listed as the number-one source of conflict in marriage. In this simple and practical guide, Dr. Gary Chapman shows couples how to work together as a team to manage their finances.

NOW WHAT?

The Chapman Guide to
Marriage After Children

AND THEN THERE WERE THREE.

Relationship expert Dr. Gary Chapman answers the age-old question, "How do we keep our marriage alive now that the children have arrived?"

MAKING LOVE

The Chapman Guide to
Making Sex an Act of Love

"LET'S MAKE LOVE." "LET'S HAVE SEX." IS THERE A DIFFERENCE? YOU BET THERE IS!

In his trademark simple, straightforward style, Dr. Chapman shows couples how to take marital intimacy to a whole new level.

Available now in stores and online!